Mascots

Mascots

By FAIRFAX DOWNEY

Illustrated by Augusto Marin

COACHWHIP PUBLICATIONS
GREENVILLE, OHIO

To

DONALD KENNICOTT

old friend and favorite editor

Mascots, by Fairfax Downey
© 2025 Coachwhip Publications edition

First published 1954
Fairfax Downey, 1893-1990
CoachwhipBooks.com

ISBN 1-61646-616-2
ISBN-13 978-1-61646-616-9

ACKNOWLEDGMENTS

THE FOLLOWING are thanked for kind permission to use material:

Phillips Wyman, publisher of *Blue Book,* to which I contributed versions of many of the mascot stories.

Maj. T. J. Edwards, author of *Military Customs* and *Mascots and Pets of the Services* (Aldershot, England, Gale & Polden, 1948 and 1953) for some of the British Army mascots.

Carl E. Trimble, 101st Airborne Division Association—"Young Abe."

Maj. Gen. P. S. Gostling, British Army, and A. MacIntosh, Ex-Pipe Major, 2nd Battalion, Scots Guards—"Bella and Bertha."

Maj. W. W. G. Redman, The Sherwood Foresters—"Derby."

Gerald D. McDonald and Laban P. Jackson—"G.I. Jenny."

Maj. Gen. Paul J. Mueller, U.S.A.—"Scrappy and Tuffy."

Brig. Gen. William W. Quinn, U.S.A., and *This Week*—"William."

Natalie Schenk—"Wahb." From *Myself and a Few Moros* by the late Lt. Col. Sydney A. Cloman, U.S.A.

Col. B. V. Ramsden and the Editor of *Army Quarterly* (British)—"Percy."

Col. Frederick P. Todd, U.S.A.R., for various suggestions.

Charles Scribner's Sons for permission to adapt the story of "Simon" from my *Cats of Destiny* (New York, 1950). That book and my *Dogs of Destiny* (1949) also contain stories of the following mascots: "Bulgarian Bell, Black Watch Cat"; "Cristobal Colon, Spanish-American War Cat"; "Moustache, French Poodle of the Napoleonic Wars"; "Boy, Prince Rupert's Poodle"; "Rin Tin Tin, World War I Mascot and Movie Star"; "Jiggs, U. S. Marine Bulldog."

FAIRFAX DOWNEY

Contents

Mascots

THE WORD *Mascot* means a bringer of good luck, and the animals and birds whose stories are told in this book were often lucky for the soldiers and sailors who adopted them. Sometimes they saved their masters' lives, fighting for them in battle. They gave companionship and pleasure to lonely men away from home in foreign lands or in camps or at sea.

Fighting men have always taken great pride in their mascots, which are as much a part of the spirit and tradition of a regiment or a crew as names of victories blazoned on flags, campaign medals, and special music played by bands. Pets, responding to the devotion shown them, have appeared to be as proud to parade behind the colors as the men in the ranks.

Mascots may be a national bird like the American eagle, or an animal like the British lion or the Welsh goat, though most of them have been dogs, because they are easier to care for and can make marches with troops. But many other kinds of beasts and birds have also served, as you will discover in the following pages.

Here are true tales of some of the most famous military mascots through the ages and of their adventures in war and peace.

Anta-m-Nekht

BATTLE LION OF RAMESES II

A LION CUB waited hungrily in a cave in the Egyptian desert for his mother to bring him food, but the lioness never returned. Hunters trapped her in a deep pit, with meat as bait, and killed her with arrows. Then they followed her tracks back to the cave and found the cub. He was small, but he fought the men savagely until they threw a net over him and tied him while he was tangled in the meshes. They took him to the royal city of Memphis on the Nile, which was the capital of Egypt, ruled by the Pharaoh Rameses II.

For days the cub snarled and clawed at anyone who came near him, but little by little he began to trust the keepers, who fed him regularly and treated him kindly. He was taken in hand by the Egyptian animal trainers, who were among the most skillful the world has ever known. They taught him to obey so well that he no longer had to be shut in a cage for safety but could be let loose. He learned many things a well-trained dog knows: to follow or stay, to hunt wild beasts and to guard a master. His training was so perfect that he was judged worthy to be given to the Pharaoh.

1

The lion was now full-grown, a magnificent tawny creature with a shaggy black mane. His trainers took him to the palace and made him understand that the Pharaoh was his new master, whose every word must be obeyed. Rameses, who had ascended the throne of Egypt in 1292 B.C. as a youth and was still a young man, was delighted with his pet. He named the lion Anta-m-Nekht, which means Mighty Repulser—one who drives away the enemies of the king. Before long the lion would live up to his name.

When the Pharaoh held court, Anta-m-Nekht crouched beside his throne. Although he acted as tame as a house cat, courtiers trembled under the glare of his yellow·eyes. Sometimes the Mighty Repulser, with a garland of flowers around his neck, marched in religious processions, for the lion was worshiped as one of the sacred animals of Egypt. But best of all he loved to hunt with his young master and run free beside the chariot horses, which had learned to overcome their natural fear of him. After the game had been surrounded by the huntsmen, Rameses would speak a sharp command that sent his lion bounding after hyena, gazelle or ostrich, to spring and bring them down with a pounce or the powerful stroke of a paw.

Anta-m-Nekht would attack men, too, at his master's order. Early in Rameses' reign the Negro tribes of Nubia to the south rebelled against the rule of Egypt. The Pharaoh led an expedition against them and took his royal beast along. When he met the enemy drawn up on the battlefield, he pointed to them and commanded his lion to charge. Roaring, Mighty Repulser rushed with such fury on the tall black spearmen that they fled

2

in terror. Egyptian archers, riding in chariots, pursued and shot down many of the rebels.

Rameses and his lion became devoted companions, and the Pharaoh decided that his pet must go with him to the next war he waged. But this time the enemy was the Hittites, and Rameses was unwilling to risk the life of his lion in battle against those fierce, hard-fighting Asiatics. He ordered his scribes to write in their records that the lion was going with him only "for pleasure and parade."

The Egyptian army, numbering twenty thousand men—charioteers and infantry—marched through Palestine and Syria. Sometimes Anta-m-Nekht trotted along beside the horses of the royal chariot, but more often he rode in a cart and was spared the fatigue of the long journey. In camp he was chained in front of his master's tent with his forepaws tied because he might jump savagely on anyone he did not know.

Unfortunately the young Pharaoh was overconfident. When he approached the Orontes River his advance guard halted to build a walled camp, while the main body of his troops was dangerously strung out along the line of march. Rameses did not suspect that the Hittite army, equal in strength to his own, was waiting in ambush behind the city of Kadesh. Suddenly three thousand Hittite chariots, each manned by three warriors, whirled out onto the plain, galloped down upon the Egyptian columns and threw them into confusion. Rameses himself, with only his bodyguard, was cut off by masses of enemy chariots.

The Pharaoh strung his bow, shouted to Menna, his charioteer, and charged at the head of his little band into the thickest of the Hittite forces. By his side in great leaping bounds ran his

3

battle lion. They crashed into the Asiatics, and above the din of combat were heard the roars of Mighty Repulser as he sprang at the throats of rearing horses and dragged screaming bowmen and spearmen from their chariots. Panic-stricken horses, completely out of their drivers' control, fled before him. Even the bravest of the Hittite warriors were filled with dismay at the sight of the great maned beast that rushed at them with gaping, bloody jaws.

Six times in three hours the battle lion followed his master in headlong charges. But hard as they and the small bodyguard fought, the Hittites were too many for them, and they would have been overcome if many of the enemy had not abandoned the attack to plunder the Egyptian camp on the plain. Once more the Pharaoh and his lion charged and broke the Hittite line, and at that moment fresh Egyptian troops arrived and turned the tide of battle.

Scribes wrote words that would be carved on stone about Rameses and his victory:

> There were thousands and hundreds of chariots round about him on all sides. He dashed them down in heaps of dead bodies before his horses. He killed all the kings and all the peoples who were allies of the Khita, together with his princes and elders, his warriors and his horses. He threw them one upon another, head over heels, into the water of the Orontes.

Then the scribes added words spoken by enemy soldiers taken prisoner:

> We were like the foals of mares, which tremble in terror at the sight of the grim lion.

4

In praise of Mighty Repulser's gallant deeds at the Battle of Kadesh, Rameses ordered that pictures of the lion also be carved on the walls of temples. Centuries passed, and the temples fell in ruins; but the carvings were saved, and they have brought the story of Anta-m-Nekht down to us through more than three thousand years.

Abul-Abbas

CHARLEMAGNE'S ELEPHANT

ABUL-ABBAS was one of the largest and strongest in the herd of hundreds of tamed and trained war elephants that belonged to the Caliph of Baghdad, Harun al-Rashid. When the great beast stamped he shook the earth, and his trumpeting could be heard for miles. When he charged into battle or marched in processions, he could carry his master and several warriors in a howdah strapped to his back, besides his driver sitting astride his neck.

His name had been given him in honor of the family of the Abbasides who reigned over Baghdad and its empire—lands that today are called Iraq and Iran and Arabia. The elephant's owner, Harun, was a wise and powerful monarch whose wonderful adventures are told in the *Arabian Nights*. But Abul-Abbas was about to face an adventure as marvelous as any of the Caliph's.

One day, in the year 800 A.D., ambassadors from Charlemagne, the mighty king of the Franks, arrived in Baghdad. Charlemagne's realm stretched over a large part of Europe, and he was called the Ruler of the West, as Harun was the Ruler of the East. Since the ambassadors had brought many splendid presents, they were asked what Charlemagne would like in return. The gift that would please him most of all, the ambassadors said, was an elephant.

At once Harun chose Abul-Abbas, towering eleven feet tall, as a gift worthy of a king whose friendship he valued. When it was time for the ambassadors to start home, the big elephant curled his trunk around his driver and lifted him up on his neck, and the caravan moved out of Baghdad, while kettle drums

thundered and trumpets blew fanfares in farewell. A difficult journey of two years stretched before them, many miles by land and by sea.

Through Asia Minor and across the deserts of North Africa they marched. Abul-Abbas could have traveled thirty or forty miles a day, but his guardians set a slow pace and treated him with the greatest care. Armed men guarded him like a treasure. Long trains of camels carried packs of his favorite foods and water-skins in case he grew thirsty between oases. Abul-Abbas always had plenty of water, not only to drink but to spray over his huge body and cool himself. In camp, canopies were put up to shade him from the sun, and attendants fanned him and whisked away flies. At every stage of the journey Isaac the Jew, the trusted courtier who was in charge, sent ahead reports by swift couriers to tell the anxious Charlemagne that his precious gift was healthy and standing the trip well.

At last they came to Carthage. A century before, in the Punic Wars between the Carthaginians and the Romans, elephants had been embarked there for the invasion of Italy. Like those big animals before him, Abul-Abbas was persuaded to go aboard a stout ship that was ready and waiting. He was chained to stanchions so that he could not shift his great weight, which might capsize the vessel. After a calm voyage across the Mediterranean, he landed at the Italian city of Pisa.

Although Hannibal the Carthaginian had taken his war elephants over the Alps in winter when he invaded Rome, Isaac would not risk the crossing with Abul-Abbas until spring. Then the big fellow climbed over the mountains easily and lumbered on northward. All along his route people came running to watch him, and they were even more excited than boys and girls are today at their first sight of an elephant in a circus parade. For nobody in Europe, except a few who had traveled in the East, had ever laid eyes on an elephant before. News of the arrival of Abul-Abbas spread everywhere, and scribes and monks as far away as Ireland described the great event in their records.

"This year for the first time," the historians wrote in Latin, "an elephant, brought from distant parts, vouchsafed the Kingdom of the Franks a wondrous spectacle. He was the gift of Harun, monarch of the Persians and ruler over all the Orient save India, who sent, besides, his friendship and made a firm alliance."

What a celebration there was when Abul-Abbas marched into Charlemagne's capital city of Aachen! The huge animal, wearing trappings of black—the royal color of the Abbasides—flapped his big ears and waved his trunk, his ivory tusks gleaming white in the sunlight. As he marched through the streets, he pulled grass from the thatched roofs of houses with that long trunk of his, which the Franks thought was like a giant's arm. His trumpeting frightened horses into running away. Nobody cared, for all the kingdom was delighted with him, Charlemagne most of all.

The big animal tore his stable apart and uprooted trees with his powerful trunk, but reached it out to take grapes gently from the King's hand. He loved to wade into the river, where he splashed and romped at his bath, squirting water over his vast body. Of course Charlemagne gave him the place of honor in his menagerie, in which lions, bears, and rare birds also were kept.

Abul-Abbas was the wonder of the zoo. People came from far and wide to convince themselves that there really was such a strange animal. Scholars arrived to study him and solve a problem that had been bothering them: Do elephants ever lie down? The learned men watched for hours, and might have had to wait longer still, since elephants, like horses, can sleep standing up. Fortunately for the observers, Abul-Abbas finally grew tired. He bent his knees, lowered his ponderous body to the ground and took a nap. Seeing was believing. The professors hurried home to write scrolls and lecture to classes about their discovery that elephants *do* lie down.

Like the white elephants of Siam, Abul-Abbas became the mascot of a kingdom. Charlemagne never risked his pet's life in battle, but showed him off everywhere. Actually Abul-Abbas was worth an army because he was living proof that his master and Harun, Ruler of the East, were friends and allies. Enemies dared not defy two such powerful monarchs who stood together.

Elephants usually have long lives, but the cold climate was hard on Abul-Abbas, and he died, still young, in 810. Charlemagne and all the Franks mourned for him. One of his tusks was carved into a hunting horn called an oliphant, like the one Roland had blown too late at the Battle of Roncesvalles, summoning Charlemagne to his aid. Roland's horn burst from his mighty blast, but the oliphant made from the tusk of Abul-Abbas survived, and you may see it today in an ancient church in Aachen.

Monsieur de Niagara

FRENCH-CANADIAN MESSENGER DOG

FIRST MARCHED a French sentry with his musket over his shoulder. An old dog followed him, and last came a puppy, trotting to keep up. They went around and around the platform behind the palisade of pointed logs which surrounded Fort Niagara in Canada. Outside in the thick forest lurked Iroquois and Seneca Indians, allies of the English who were striving hard, in those late years of the 1600's, to drive the French away and win the rich fur trade of Canada for themselves. If the sentry and his dogs did not keep a sharp watch, the Indians might capture the fort and kill all its garrison.

The puppy tried to act exactly like the older dog, his father. If the old dog stood on his hind legs to look over the palisade, the puppy leaped up with stretching forepaws too, though he was still not tall enough to see over the top. If the father heard a sound in the forest and growled a warning, the son imitated him with a small, squeaky growl. The soldier grinned at the little fellow but praised him for learning to be a good watch-dog.

13

The old dog was named Vingt Sols after the twenty French coins which his master, Lieutenant Raymond-Blaise des Bergères, an officer of the garrison, had paid for him. The puppy's name was Monsieur de Niagara after the fort guarding the Niagara River, which connects Lakes Ontario and Erie.

When Vingt Sols grew old and died, Monsieur de Niagara took over his duties. He stood guard with the sentinels. His keen ears could hear savage warriors creeping through the woods, or even the slight sounds they made when they tried to slip up by paddling canoes across the river. No Iroquois or Senecas succeeded in surprising the fort while Monsieur de Niagara was on guard. But in 1688 so many soldiers of the garrison died of scurvy that Fort Niagara had to be abandoned.

Lieutenant des Bergères was ordered to another fort—at Chambly—and of course he took his dog with him. During the long, lonely months Monsieur de Niagara was wonderful, cheery company. Many a night the French officer sat down and wrote affectionately in his diary about his pet and all they had done that day together. The soldiers also made much of the dog, the only one in the garrison, and adopted him as their mascot.

But Monsieur de Niagara, happy though he was with men who loved him, grew lonesome for his own kind. One day he ran off through the woods looking for other dogs, and instinct led him to the neighboring fort of La Prairie de la Madelaine. Soon he heard barking and raced in through the gate. While he was making friends with the dogs there, a soldier recognized him as the Chambly dog, caught him and led him to the Commandant.

14

They thought Monsieur de Niagara might have been with troops coming from the other stockade. His arrival alone could mean that the men had been waylaid and wiped out by Indians, and only the dog had escaped.

The Commandant at La Prairie was worried, but he had only enough soldiers to guard the fort and did not dare to send any out as a searching party. Suddenly a bright idea struck him. He wrote a note to Lieutenant des Bergères and tied it to Monsieur de Niagara's collar. Then the officer fed the dog, put him outside the stockade and told him to go home.

But Monsieur de Niagara did not care to go home at the moment. He liked it where he was. The soldiers had to cut switches and threaten to whip him before he would leave. The dog gave them a look which said as plainly as words: "Why do you treat a visitor, who was only making a friendly call, so badly?" Then he put his tail between his legs and loped off through the forest.

Lieutenant des Bergères gladly welcomed back his truant pet. While the dog, tail wagging frantically, was leaping up on his master, the officer caught sight of the note attached to his collar. He unfastened it and read it. What better way of answering it could there be than sending the reply by the same messenger? Monsieur de Niagara was fed, and a letter, which said that all was well at Chambly, took the place of the one he had brought. Then he was chased out of the fort to run back to La Prairie.

It must have seemed a strange business to Monsieur de Niagara—all that shuttling back and forth between the two forts! But the soldiers at both places petted him, called him a good

15

dog and gave him plenty to eat, so he always obeyed. He carried many messages, dashing past watchful Indians who would surely have shot down a human courier. Monsieur de Niagara, fast and clever, always got through safely, though often he had to dodge arrows.

Monsieur de Niagara's *poste à patand*—postal service on the paw—was so valuable that his master claimed a special ration allowance for him. The Intendant at Quebec promptly granted it and ordered that the dog be listed as a member of the French army in America. When the roll was called, and Monsieur de Niagara heard his name, he would give a loud bark that meant "Here." If he were absent, a soldier would answer for him, "*En*

16

course" or "À *la chasse*," which explained that he was away carrying a message or that he was out hunting.

For several years after he died, soldiers still answered for him when his name was called. That was partly in honor of his memory and partly because hungry troopers wanted the extra ration that was still being issued for their old pet.

Monsieur de Niagara was the first messenger dog in North America. Many years later, in the First and Second World Wars, brave dogs like him carried messages for the American and other armies.

Billy

GOAT OF THE ROYAL WELSH FUSILIERS

WHEN THE Royal Welsh Fusiliers crossed the Atlantic in 1775 as part of the British army sent by King George III to halt the rebellion in the American Colonies, the soldiers of that famed regiment brought with them their handsome white goat, Billy. The Royal Welsh, called Fusiliers because they once carried guns known as fusils, had had long-haired goats like this one as their mascots ever since the regiment was formed in 1689, and all the goats had been named Billy.

The regiment was stationed in Boston, and, although there had been trouble in that town between British troops and Americans, the Fusiliers could not let March 1st go by without a celebration. It was St. David's Day, as great an occasion for any Welshman as St. Patrick's Day is for the Irish.

Drummer boys gave Billy a bath, dried him and combed his silky hair. A sergeant, called the Goat-Major, gilded the animal's curved horns and hung on his forehead a silver plaque marked with the name of King George, who had given Billy to the regiment. Next came a halter and an embroidered blanket. Last a bunch of onionlike leeks, the national vegetable of Wales, was fastened between the goat's horns where he could not nibble them, though he tried his best.

Now Billy was dressed and ready for his entrance. Drums beat and fifers struck up an old tune, "Of Noble Race Was Shenkin." Billy, led by the Goat-Major and followed by the musicians, marched into the mess room where the officers were

having dinner. His pace was stately and his behavior perfect until a drummer boy climbed onto his back. Then Billy suddenly turned just as rebellious as the American Colonists. With a mighty leap he landed on the table and tossed his rider off into the dishes. Chinaware crashed, and Billy knocked over glasses and candlesticks. As he cavorted along the table, officers

19

grabbed for him but dodged back to keep from being butted. Bleating and tossing his horns, Billy jumped through a window and dashed through the streets of Boston. Passing citizens cheered him loudly, and it was a long time before soldiers could catch him.

Billy was quiet when he watched his regiment march off to fight at Lexington and Concord, and quieter still after the Battle of Bunker Hill. Many of the Royal Welsh were killed there, and Billy missed his old friends. He served throughout the Revolution, and after the surrender at Yorktown he returned with the Fusiliers to England. There, an honored veteran, he finally died of old age.

Other Billies followed him. One perished of the cold in the freezing weather of the Crimean War, and another was killed in action during the Indian Mutiny. Later Billies were presented to the regiment by Queen Victoria from her herd of fine Kashmir goats at Windsor, and the Fusiliers became prouder than ever of their mascots.

When the regiment formed separate battalions, each was given a goat. The Billy of a battalion in India in 1900 rode in style in a small cart pulled by white oxen, and awed natives of the villages believed he was a god worshiped by the British. This goat was a stubborn creature, and, though he consented to march at the head of the column in church and other parades, he balked at any distance over a mile.

When Billy was tied in front of his own small tent, he would slip his tether whenever he sighted an Indian selling vegetables. After a stealthy stalk he would take his victim in the rear, deliver a terrific butt and scatter the man's wares. Not until that moment would the Goat-Major appear to round up his charge. Every soldier in the battalion believed there was perfect understanding between Billy and his keeper, because the two of them were often seen sharing the vegetables.

The First Battalion of the Fusiliers left its white mascot at home when it went to fight in Burma in 1943 during the Second World War. When St. David's Day arrived, there seemed to be no way to celebrate it properly—no goat, no leeks, no drum. Hastily the Fusiliers found and bought a native goat. His dirty hide was black and white, but they washed him thoroughly, painted his black spots white and put a big pair of false horns over his own small ones. Then they got hold of onions in place of leeks, and a tom-tom was used for a drum. The new Billy was led around to visit each company until he grew tired. Then soldiers carried him. So St. David was duly honored after all.

Today there is a handsome white Billy on duty as usual with the Royal Welsh Fusiliers. He is the father of small Billies who will grow up to be hard-butting mascots of a hard-fighting regiment.

The Blue Hen's Chickens

GAMECOCKS OF THE DELAWARE REGIMENT

IT WAS ALWAYS an event in Kent County, Delaware, when
small eggs in the nest of the Blue Hen were hatched. Some of
her chicks were certain to grow up into especially fine gamecocks, brave little roosters that love to fight.

Larger chickens only quarrel and peck one another now and
then, but gamecocks have not changed much since they were
wild jungle birds thousands of years ago. They have been
tamed, but they are still fierce when they fight each other for
the fun of it, as some men, some dogs and a few other animals
do. Gamecocks will battle each other in the barnyard, and fight
just as willingly when their owners match them in a ring.

Perhaps the Blue Hen's slate-blue feathers came from a breed
of game chickens that crossed the Atlantic on a British frigate
as pets of the crew. But in 1776 she was being called an American rather than an English bird, because the country where she
lived had declared its independence and become the United
States. Strange as it seems, two chickens of her latest brood
were going to help Americans win their freedom in the Revolution.

These two gamecocks were chosen as mascots by the Kent

22

County men of Captain Jonathan Caldwell's company, part of the regiment called the Delaware Blues because of the color of their uniforms. Soon the whole regiment, commanded by Colonel John Haslet, adopted the little roosters. They were given no names of their own but simply called the Blue Hen's Chickens after their mother. When they went to war with the Delaware troops, they were about two years old, and their tail feathers, hackles and combs had been clipped to put them into fighting trim.

The Delaware Blues were part of the army General George Washington assembled on Long Island to keep the British, sailing down from Canada, from capturing New York. There the Delaware men met other regiments who also had gamecocks. Quickly matches were arranged to find out whose birds were the best fighters.

Handlers knelt inside rings of crowding soldiers and held the little roosters beak to beak. It was always the Blue Hen's Chickens that pecked most furiously at the other cocks. The second they were released, they flew into the air and struck lightning blows with their spurred heels. Even if the fight went against them at first, they never gave up. They were so game—so full of courage—that they rushed back to the attack and downed their opponents or chased them out of the ring. Then the tiny creatures flapped their wings and uttered shrill crows of triumph. The Delaware soldiers cheered them and boasted:

"We're sons of the old Blue Hen and we're game to the end!"

It wasn't only a boast. The Delaware men proved they could equal the bravery their gamecocks had shown. When the Americans were beaten at the Battle of Long Island, the Blues stood

24

firm and covered the retreat. At White Plains they fought a gallant rearguard action along with the Marylanders and drove back the British pursuit. Captain Caldwell was wounded, but he insisted on staying on duty in command of his company.

The valor of the Blues, like that of their gamecocks, spread their fame, and soon not only Haslet's regiment but all Delaware troops were known in the American army as the Blue Hen's Chickens. It was not the first time that such small, plucky roosters had helped inspire a fighting spirit in soldiers. Many hundreds of years before, Greek forces marching against a much stronger Persian army and expecting to be defeated halted by the roadside to watch a pair of gamecocks battling. The Greeks were so stirred by the courage of the birds that they won a great victory over the enemy, and after that cockfights were made a part of the Athenian games.

Colonel Haslet of the Blues gave a splendid example of bravery. When Washington crossed the Delaware to surprise the Hessians at Trenton, Colonel Haslet fell into the icy river while he was landing his men. Yet he fought through the next day in spite of the painful swelling of his frostbitten legs. The sick man received orders relieving him from active duty, but he put the orders in his pocket so he would not miss the Battle of Princeton. There he was killed by a British bullet. His regiment, reduced to less than one hundred men, was disbanded, and the surviving soldiers and the Blue Hen's Chickens joined other troops.

Stories of the gamecocks were passed down by veterans to their sons, and poems were written celebrating them. In 1930, Delaware made the Blue Hen its state bird.

Kentucky

PIG OF THE WAR OF 1812

A COMPANY of American volunteers, marching to invade Canada in the War of 1812, halted and broke ranks near the town of Harrodsburg, Kentucky. Combat with the British lay ahead of them, but that would have to wait. Right here in front of them by the roadside a fight was raging, a scrap a man seldom had a chance to see. It was a battle royal between two furious pigs.

None of the spectators could guess how the argument had started. In a sty it might have begun with one pig's shoving the other away from the trough, or it could have been a quarrel over the best mud puddle to wallow in. But this mix-up by the road was a good, clean fight, a heavyweight championship bout. The big porkers tore into each other, grunting, pushing and biting. At last one of them rolled the other over in the dust and drove him away, the beaten pig squealing at the top of his lungs.

The soldiers, cheering the victor, expected him to walk off in triumph. But to their surprise and vast amusement he fol-

lowed them when they resumed their march. Evidently this fighting pig had taken a liking to the fighting men from his own state.

The pig, heavy though he was, did not waddle. He marched right along with the men. That night when the troops made camp he hollowed out a bed in leaves for himself and settled down. In the morning he turned out for reveille, took his place on the flank of the column and stepped out when the command to march was given. After that, Kentucky, as the new mascot was named, was considered a member of the company. He was issued regular rations even though, naturally enough, he "ate like a pig."

Across the route of the column lay the Ohio River. When the Kentuckians reached its bank, they said good-by to their mascot. Let him find his way back home now. There were many miles still to march, and not a man believed a pig would be able to cover such a long distance. They patted Kentucky's fat back and shooed him away as they boarded barges to ferry them across the river.

They found out that they had vastly underrated their volunteer mascot. Looking back from the boats in midstream, the soldiers saw Kentucky plunge into the Ohio and swim strongly after them. They had heard that pigs couldn't swim, because they would cut their throats with the sharp hoofs of their short forelegs when they made strokes. But that yarn plainly wasn't true of Kentucky. Floating beautifully and paddling strongly, he plowed through the water faster than the men could row the barges. He was waiting on the farther shore when his friends landed.

Kentucky never lagged behind as the column pushed on to

join General William Henry Harrison and its own commander, Isaac Shelby, a veteran of the Revolution and the Governor of Kentucky. Food ran short, but none of the men was willing to slaughter the pig, several hundred pounds of handy pork. He was their "fellow soldier," they said, and they shared their own dwindling rations with their mascot.

At Lake Erie the Kentuckians embarked on Captain Oliver Hazard Perry's American ships, which had won a great victory over a British fleet. But when they landed on Bass Island their mascot pig turned obstinate. That was as far as he was going, and there he stayed. His friends laughed and said he must have read the Constitution and known that it forbade volunteer forces crossing a border into a foreign country unless they had been mustered into the federal service.

So Kentucky missed the Battle of the Thames, where the Americans defeated a British army and its Indian allies and killed Chief Tecumseh. But the pig was waiting on American soil when his friends came back, and he trotted to his regular place on the flank for the march home. Now it was winter, and Kentucky suffered greatly, slipping and sliding along the icy roads. He made it as far as the Ohio River, but there, completely exhausted, he stopped and lay down.

Governor Shelby asked a farmer to take care of the faithful animal, and Kentucky stayed on the farm for the rest of the war. When the peace treaty was signed, he was not forgotten. The Governor sent for him and had him brought to the Shelby estate, which was called "Traveller's Rest."

For Kentucky no home could have a better name. He had traveled far and deserved a rest. He took one in a comfortable sty with plenty to eat as long as he lived.

29

Mexique

AMERICAN ARMY MULE

ONE DAY in 1832 a young lieutenant strode through an army camp in Alabama. He was William Tecumseh Sherman, who in the Civil War would become a famous Union general and fight his way through the heart of the Confederacy to Atlanta and on to the sea. Now, as he passed the stables, he stopped to look at a big sorrel mule tied outside on the picket line. The mule lifted his head and brayed. That long, raucous heehaw of his was inherited from his donkey father, as were his long ears, while his body was like that of his mother, a mare.

Sherman stood admiring this splendid specimen of army mule. Such a strong fellow would surely pull more than his share in a team hauling a heavily laden supply wagon mile after mile, and he could easily carry on his back a pack weighing two hundred and fifty pounds or more. Sherman called the stable sergeant, to question him about the animal. Yes, the sergeant agreed, the mule was a wonder, although he was no longer a youngster. Why, some veterans in the garrison said that this mule had joined the army away back in 1818 during General Andrew Jackson's campaign against the Seminole Indians in

30

Florida. There were probably years of work in him still—how many years nobody would have dared to predict.

Somehow the memory of that mule stuck in Sherman's mind. Other officers and soldiers, too, often remembered him in spite of the hundreds or thousands of army mules they saw. It was partly the mule's unusual sorrel color—most mules are dark brown—that set him apart, but most memorable were his reputation as a willing and faithful worker, and the way he stayed on duty year after year.

It was in the war with Mexico in 1847 that the mule won his name of Mexique. He was still going strong in the Civil War and in the Indian-fighting years. Mexique never seemed to grow old. He kept on hauling supply wagons and army ambulances.

In corrals he looked down his long nose at young mule recruits from Missouri, whose tails were shaved to distinguish them from old-timers like himself. (Their name of "shavetails" was also given to new second lieutenants, who are still called that today.)

Mexique was present for duty at Mount Vernon Barracks, near Mobile, Alabama, in 1883. By that time he had an extraordinary record of fifty or perhaps even sixty years of service behind him. Mules hardly ever live so long. Mexique was stiff and creaky in his joints, and his hair had turned entirely white, but he still did a little light work. Most of the time, though, he was allowed to wander free around the post as the beloved mascot of the garrison.

Then came an order that old, worn-out army animals must be sold. Mexique's friends, alarmed and upset, at once banded together to save him. They wrote a letter, promising to buy the mule with their own money if the government would continue to stable and feed him.

By good luck the letter reached an old admirer of Mexique, William Tecumseh Sherman, who was now the Commanding General of the U.S. Army. It was forty years since he had seen the mule, but he warmly remembered the veteran animal. He took up his pen and wrote these words:

> I have seen that mule, and whether true or false, the soldiers believe he was left at Big Springs, where the Mount Vernon Barracks now are, at the time General Jackson's army camped there about 1819 or 1820. Tradition says he was once a sorrel; but is now white with age. The Quartermaster's Department will be chargeable with ingratitude if that mule is sold or the maintenance of it is thrown on the charitable officers of the post. I advise he be kept in the Department, fed and main-

32

tained till death. I think the mule was at Fort Morgan, Mobile Point, when I was there in 1842.

General Sherman's letter was then sent on to Secretary of War Robert Todd Lincoln, son of President Abraham Lincoln. Without hesitation the Secretary ordered: "Let this mule be well kept and cared for at the public expense as long as he lives."

By the time this order, signed with the famous names of Lincoln and Sherman, reached the post, Mexique had been sold. But it was his army friends who had bought him with the highest bid.

Mexique lived nearly three years longer, "turned out never to be harnessed again, to roll at his own sweet will and to be furnished a full ration till time with him shall be no more."

Donald

THE BLACK WATCH'S DEER

DONALD WAS a young deer, with horns that were no more than sprigs, when he joined the Black Watch at its barracks in Edinburgh, Scotland, one day in 1836. He was a new sort of mascot for that celebrated regiment, which had had a dog in the wars with Napoleon and a cat in the Crimean War. But Donald suited the Watch splendidly, for he would grow up to be a great Highland stag, a favorite Scottish animal.

Young as he was, Donald soon showed that he was no pet that needed to be pampered and coddled. He made a three-day march with the troops, and every evening picked out a spot for his lair. If it happened to block the way to the regiment's campsite, Donald wouldn't move. The Watch had to detour around him. But he was a real help at drills, where he acted as a military policeman and pushed spectators back to the edges of the parade ground.

Before long, Donald made up his mind that he belonged in parades himself. Without any training or urging he stepped out and took his place at the side of the sergeant-major. Bagpipes skirled and drums beat. Off marched the Highlanders in swing-

34

ing kilts of black, green and blue tartan, dark colors that had given them their name of the Black Watch. Donald, striding along in front, was a proud sight that drew cheers from every onlooker.

After that day, he was never absent from his position at parades, drills or route marches. He attended field days, too, though he didn't care for scouting and target practice, and would wander away. But he listened for bugles sounding the recall and dashed back a mile or so at full speed, in time to march back to barracks.

Donald was a little late one day at a big review in which various troops besides the Black Watch were taking part. He trotted hastily out onto the parade ground and posted himself at the head of the column of another Scottish regiment, the 72nd Highlanders. Then he glanced around and saw that he had made a mistake. Donald looked annoyed and turned stubborn. He would not march with these strange soldiers, nor would he let them march. He refused to budge and held up the entire 72nd until its colonel ordered a deer-drive to herd him back to the Black Watch.

Donald was full-grown, with a magnificent spread of antlers, when the Watch moved to Dublin. Whenever the regiment marched through the crowded city streets, Donald stalked ahead to clear the way, and usually people scattered before him. But one day a tough Irishman, who didn't like deer or Scots, stood defiantly in the middle of the street and would not stir a step. Donald snorted, lowered his horns and charged. The Irishman uttered a wild yelp of terror, whirled and ran at top speed. He barely managed to escape the threatening antlers close behind

35

him by dodging through the crowd and scrambling over a wall.

That evening Donald's owners trimmed and blunted the points of his horns. But they were still deadly weapons. He only had to shake them warningly, and traffic gave him the right of way.

Donald made friends with one other regiment besides his own —the Scots Greys, cavalrymen who shared their horses' oats and straw with him. But the Greys were ordered away to another station, and their place was taken by the Bays, also cavalry. These newcomers were stingy with feed and bedding, and turned Donald out of their stables. The angry deer declared war and chased any Bay trooper he caught out in the open. The

Black Watch, delighted with their mascot's spirit, made a chalk drawing on a wall of their mess hall. It showed Donald pinning one of his cavalry enemies against a building with his horns. Underneath the sketch was written: "The Stag at Bay."

Donald made a nine-day march from Dublin to Limerick with his regiment in 1839. Although he was footsore and weary each night, he was not too tired to keep the stablemen respectful at the inns where he was given a stall. He let them know that he was an important member of the Black Watch and must be treated with the consideration his dignity deserved.

When the Black Watch was ordered on foreign service it seemed best not to take Donald along. The big stag would be hard to handle on shipboard and might be injured if the transport rolled and pitched in a storm. Arrangements were made to retire him and send him to live in freedom in the forest of a nobleman's estate.

The day of parting was a sad one. It took a squad of husky, reluctant soldiers to tie up the strong animal with ropes and load him onto a wagon. Donald knew very well what was happening to him—that he was being taken away from the regiment he loved. His cries were pitiful, and it was even said that great teardrops welled from his beseeching brown eyes. Donald's comrades were as grief-stricken as he. They were not ashamed of the moisture hard fists rubbed from their own eyes as they saw the wagon roll away.

In 1862 an officer visited the estate to inquire after the mascot. He was told that Donald, as soon as he was first released, had bounded off to the most remote part of the forest and there made his lair summer and winter. Donald would have nothing to do with men who were not soldiers, nor with mere civilian deer who had never had the honor of leading the Black Watch on parade. Since he was dangerous to anyone who dared come near him, orders were unwillingly given to have him shot.

Donald could not have been sorry to leave his wild, lonely life. The Black Watch had been the only friends he ever knew, and with them only had he found happiness. His faithful and devoted career will never be forgotten, for it is a worthy part of the history of a famous regiment.

Jacob

GOOSE OF THE COLDSTREAM GUARDS

A SENTRY PACED up and down at the gate of a farm near Quebec, Canada, one autumn day in 1838. His name was John Kemp, and he belonged to a famous regiment, the Coldstream Guards, which had been sent from England to help put down a rebellion of French-Canadians against the British government. A small detachment of Kemp's battalion was guarding the farm, because it was suspected to be a meeting place for the rebels; but there had been no trouble, and all was quiet.

While the Guardsman walked his post, he watched a plump white goose waddling across the barnyard. Suddenly a fox jumped from the bushes and darted after the goose. The bird squawked in terror and fled, with the fox hot after it and gaining at every bound. Private Kemp, who had been a farmer before he enlisted in the army, raised his musket to shoot the fox, then lowered it. He dared not fire; for his comrades would think the shot was a warning of an enemy attack.

The goose, wings flapping frantically and short legs scuttling, dashed straight toward the soldier for protection. But the fox was so hungry that he had lost all fear of man. He snapped at the goose's tailfeathers, and was about to seize his prey when Kemp killed him with a bayonet thrust.

The white goose showed his gratitude as eloquently as any creature could. He rubbed his head against the legs of the man who had saved his life and made little quacking sounds that expressed his thanks as plainly as words. Then he took his place beside the Guardsman and solemnly patrolled with him. When the next sentry came on duty, the goose stayed and marched back and forth with him and with later reliefs as well.

Kemp and his comrades named the goose Jacob and made a pet of him. But Jacob remembered his duty. Every day and all day he marched beside the sentries at the farm gate. The Coldstreams laughed and said that Jacob found the sentry box a safer refuge from foxes than the barnyard was. But sentinels grow lonely, and they were as glad of the goose's company as he was of theirs.

Two months passed by. On a cold November night, Private Kemp was again standing guard at the gate. Jacob, when it grew dark, usually went to roost in the barn, but tonight he would not leave his favorite Guardsman. For an hour the soldier paced up and down the path he had beaten in the snow, the goose stepping faithfully along at his heels. A storm was brewing, and clouds, scudding across the sky from time to time, dimmed the light of a bright moon.

Abruptly the sentry halted and brought his musket to port arms. He thought he had heard a noise above the ghostly wailing of the wind through the branches of the trees.

"Who goes there?" he challenged in a loud voice.

There was no answer. Reassured, the sentry grounded his

40

gun and stood at ease. He must have imagined that he heard something. As time passed and nothing happened, he had to struggle to keep awake.

Dark shadows lengthened on the snowy field behind the sentry box. A band of rebels had slipped out of the woods, and two of them were creeping up to surprise the sleepy sentinel. Their footfalls muffled by the snow, they closed in on him from both sides. Knives upraised, they jumped for his throat.

A whirring white shape swept up from the ground and flung itself in their faces. It was Jacob, valiantly defending the man to whom he owed his life. His wings beat about the heads of the attackers, blinding them and driving them staggering backward. Before they could recover, the Guardsman sprang into action, bayoneted one and fired at the other, who fled in panic. By this time, on the heels of their scouts, the whole rebel band had come up and were closing in. Jacob charged them, hissing like a serpent, and they retreated before the goose's sharp beak and the sentry's swinging musket. Then the main guard, alerted by the sound of the shot, came up at a run and routed the raiders.

Now it was Kemp's turn to be grateful—to stroke Jacob's ruffled feathers, praise him and feed him favorite tidbits. Word of the goose's courage spread, and he became the hero of the battalion. The Coldstreams bought a golden gorget, the small piece of armor knights once wore to protect their throats, and hung it around Jacob's neck as a decoration for bravery.

Still another honor came to Jacob when the Coldstream Guards listed him on muster rolls as a "friend," the affectionate title they give their official mascot. When they left Canada, they took him home to England, and at headquarters in London Jacob took up his round of duties with sentries at the barracks gates. A goose mounting guard with a crack regiment of the British Army was a strange sight, but to everyone who learned Jacob's story it was touching and heartwarming. Nobody ever questioned the gallant goose's right to march with the troops he loved.

Year after year Jacob turned out with the guard. Before reporting at his post he took a dip in his special circular bird bath and preened his feathers until they gleamed as white as the crossbelts over the scarlet jackets of his companions. Back and forth he strutted with a stiff, highly military gait—a gait exactly like the one used by soldiers on parade and called the "goose step." When the sentry saluted an officer or the colors, Jacob also stiffened to attention. Children, of whom he was very fond, flocked to watch him and give him good things to eat. But he would accept only when he and the sentry were "standing easy" and regulations allowed him to relax.

In time Jacob was given a deserved promotion and raised to the rank of superintendent of sentinels. A great British general, the Duke of Wellington, praised him for his long and faithful devotion to duty.

One day during his twelfth year of service, Jacob, marching through a narrow gateway, was run over by a wagon. Doctors tried to save him but they could do nothing. "He died," the newspapers said, "like a true English soldier at his post of duty." The body of the goose was buried with full military honors. His head was mounted on a plaque which is still displayed today in the Coldstreams' orderly room at Whitehall, between flags the regiment carried at the Battle of Waterloo. Around the feathered neck hangs the golden gorget, won for bravery in Canada. On it are the words: "Jacob, 2nd Battalion, Coldstream Guards. Died on duty."

Dick

DOG OF OLD IRONSIDES

DICK FOLLOWED his master, an American sailor, through the streets of Callao, Peru. He was a lively, friendly dog, part spaniel. Dick wagged the tail that curved jauntily over his back when he and his master met another bluejacket.

While the two men talked, Dick lay panting from the heat and looking up at them. He knew from the way they glanced down at him that they must be talking about him. His owner, a seaman on the brig *Corsair,* was offering to give the dog to his friend. It would be hard to part with his pet, but space on the *Corsair* was cramped, and his friend was carpenter on another ship, with a shop where Dick would have plenty of room and soft wood shavings for his bed.

So Dick changed masters, and that evening was rowed out to the most famous ship in the American navy, the U.S.S. *Constitution.* He was carried up a ladder against her oaken hull, a hull so stout that it had won her the name of Old Ironsides when British cannonballs bounced off it in the War of 1812. It was now the year 1840, but the fine frigate was still strong and seaworthy for the peacetime cruise on which she was bound.

Regulations stated that no dogs were allowed aboard, but Dick was kept hidden till the ship sailed. When officers found him he wagged that perky tail of his and stretched up his sleek head to be petted. The crew, seeing the captain lean down to pat him, knew Dick had made a firm friend and wouldn't be put ashore.

Dick quickly showed he was a seagoing dog and knew his duties. He had learned on the *Corsair* that when drums beat the quarters it was a signal for the crew to rush to their battle stations. The minute the drummers began their roll Dick scampered away, darting past the hurrying sailors or running between their legs. He was always first at his post, which he had decided was the gun deck. There he took his stand and saluted the gunnery lieutenant with a tailwag.

One day, when the *Constitution* anchored off an island and boats were lowered to give the crew shore liberty, Dick jumped down into the first one and took a seat in the bow. Nearing the beach, he leaped overboard, swam ashore and waited to be rowed back. He repeated the performance, barking joyously, with each boatload.

Dick would crouch on a boom and with great interest watch sailors polishing the decks with holystones. If any help was needed, he was ready and willing, his shipmates said.

> Why, when they passed the word for holystoning decks (a grinning sailor reported) and the captain of the fore-top began to complain because someone had stolen all his holystones, Dick was standing by. No sooner had he heard it than off he starts full trot, dives down to the berth-deck and muzzles two stones belonging to the cooks. Though the master-at-arms and ship's corporal chased him hard, armed with a couple of belaying pins, he reached the gangway safely with those articles in his mouth. Most curious part of it was those holystones were marked "fore-top starboard," too.

The crew declared that Dick was just as attentive to his duty when sails were being reefed. One of his bluejacket friends told this yarn about him:

> While our watch was putting the ship about, in the hurry and hustle they forgot to send a man to the jib-sheet. At the word "helm's-a-lee" I ran to the lee side, and there was Dick as busy as could be in a gale of wind, clearing away the sheet with his mouth. He had all the turns off the pin but one.

47

Perhaps all the stories told about Dick weren't quite true, but he was a very smart dog. His affection and pranks did much to make Old Ironsides a happy ship. Once he went along with the carpenter and his mates who were going ashore to put up a target for gunnery practice. When the target was in place, the men withdrew out of range, and the cannon fired. Dick scurried back through the sand, chasing each cannonball that fell short until it rolled to a standstill. The way he placed his forepaws on it as soon as it cooled and barked triumphantly—just as if it were a play ball thrown for him to fetch—made all the crew laugh.

But one day, while the *Constitution* was cruising off the coast of South America, anxious word sped through the ship that Dick had disappeared. All hands turned out to search for him between decks, in sick bay and galley, through boats swinging at the davits. The sailors even climbed the masts to look in the tops. At last they sadly acknowledged that he must have fallen overboard from the boom or a risky perch in the forechains as the frigate went about sharply in a strong wind.

As a tribute from the whole crew, Fore-top-man Henry James Mercier wrote a story including this poem in memory of Dick:

> Yes, when we made that slippery bend,
> Had you but gave a bark, my friend,
> You'd found each tar with a rope's end
>   To heave to you;
> And every one their aid would lend
>   Amongst our crew.
>
> But, alas! no helping hand was nigh,
> No friendly shipmate standing by,

48

No ear to catch your drowning cry
    Or plaintive moans;
For if there were you would not lie
    With Davy Jones.

And when some future years pass by,
And other ships our tars may try,
Your praise from group to group will fly,
    And that full quick;
And many a salt will mournful cry,
    "Alas! poor Dick."

Today the *Constitution*, a ship glorious in American history, lies docked in Boston harbor, and you may go aboard and walk her famous decks. If you do, remember that on those oaken planks once trotted a little dog the crew of Old Ironsides loved.

Bob

SCOTS GUARDS' TERRIER

WHY WOULD A DOG, born in a butcher shop, where there are plenty of scraps of meat for dinner, ever want to leave home? Bob's master, the butcher, could not understand why his black-and-white terrier kept wandering away. One day he followed the dog through the streets and found him in the barracks of the Scots Guards who were on duty at Windsor, Queen Victoria's castle. The butcher led his pet back, but next day Bob was gone again. Like many other dogs, he loved soldiers. There were always some of those tall men in scarlet uniforms who were not too busy to pet him and play with him. Their cooks fed him as generously as the butcher did, and Bob's appetite was bigger than ever because of the exercise he got marching with the Guard.

Bob was picked up and taken home often, but each time he was soon back at the barracks again. When the Scots were ordered from Windsor to Chobham Camp, the butcher gave up

50

and let his dog go. Bob was promptly appointed the official mascot and marched off proudly at the head of his regiment.

When the Crimean War broke out in 1854, the Scots Guards were among the British troops sent to fight as allies of the French and Turks against the Russians. Bob, boarding the transport with his regiment, almost lost his life. Some cruel soldiers who didn't know him took him for a stray dog, and were about to throw him overboard when the Scots rushed to his rescue. The Guardsmen were so angry that they nearly tossed Bob's enemies into the sea instead.

The terrier landed with his masters for a few days of shore leave at the Bulgarian port of Varna. After being cooped up on a rolling ship, it was good to be on steady land again, and Bob enjoyed running through the streets of the town. There were interesting sights to be seen and even more interesting smells to be sniffed. Also there were Bulgarian dogs to be chased if they failed to show proper respect to a fighting British terrier. During his busy tour Bob lost the Guardsmen he had been following, but he kept his eyes open, and when he saw soldiers drifting toward the docks he knew it was time to go aboard. He loped down to the waterfront and trotted up a gangway. But he had boarded the wrong ship.

No sooner was Bob missed than the Colonel of the Scots Guards sent officers with orders to find the mascot and bring him back, if they had to search the whole fleet. Bob was found and returned to his own regiment, wagging his tail and looking very pleased with all the attention he was given.

Hard fighting awaited the British army in the Crimea. During

51

the confusion of the Battle of Alma, Bob disappeared again, but now his regiment, hurrying forward, could spare no time to look for him. Somehow he managed to follow the trail of the Scots and join them at Balaclava, where the gallant Six Hundred of the Light Brigade made their disastrous charge.

At the siege of Sevastopol, Bob proved that he had become a veteran. He took his turn standing guard with sentries in the front-line trenches and growled warnings whenever he heard Russian scouts. During the bitter cold weather, which caused much sickness and suffering among the troops, the terrier's cheerful, lively company was a great blessing to his friends.

Bob took part in the hard-fought Battle of Inkerman. As the Russian guns opened fire, and cannonballs, falling short, rolled toward the Scots, Bob dashed out and chased them, barking furiously. Those rolling iron things were meant to hurt his comrades of the Guard, and he wasn't going to let them do it if he could stop them. One of the cannonballs was still red-hot, and he burned his nose badly when he tried to bite it. That was his only wound of the war.

In 1856, after the Allies won the victory, Bob sailed back to England and marched proudly at the head of the Scots Guards when they paraded in London. He was decorated with the Crimean Medal and posed with three Guardsmen for a painting which was called "Four Old Campaigners."

It was strange that Bob's life, which began in a butcher shop, should end the way it did. One day, while he was marching with the Guard, he was run over and killed by a butcher's cart.

Officers of the regiment had Bob's skin stuffed and placed in the Scottish United Services Museum at Edinburgh Castle. Sir Francis Hastings Doyle wrote this poem in his honor:

'Tis sad that after all these years,
    Our comrade and our friend,
The brave dog of the Fusiliers,
    Should meet with such an end.

Up Alma's hill, among the vines,
    We laughed to see him trot,
Then frisk along the silent lines
    To chase the rolling shot. . . .

Marked by the medal, his of right,
    And by his kind, keen face,
Under the visionary light
    Poor Bob shall keep his place.

Derby

RAM OF THE SHERWOOD FORESTERS

"DO YOU THINK you could capture that ram?"

An officer of the Sherwood Foresters turned to a tall grenadier and pointed to a big black ram, tethered in the courtyard of a temple in the Indian town of Kotah. It was during the terrible Mutiny of 1858, when British troops were fighting hard to conquer Sepoys, native soldiers who had rebelled. A strong force of Sepoys was using the temple as a fort, and capturing the ram under its walls would be a highly dangerous feat. But the Foresters were hungry and needed meat badly.

The grenadier, Private Cody, looked where the officer's fingers pointed.

"Yes, sir, I'm sure I could get that ram," he answered.

"Right-o. Go ahead," the officer ordered.

Cody crept forward and climbed over the yard fence. Mutineers spotted him and began to fire, but he took time to pat and make friends with the ram before he untied him. Then he picked the heavy animal up in his arms and ran. A storm of bullets whizzed around the gallant grenadier, but he dashed back safely to his own lines.

55

The Sherwood Foresters cheered their comrade and admired his prize. Though they had meant to have the ram for dinner, he was such a fine-looking fellow that they could not bear to butcher him. He reminded them of rams at home in the English county of Derbyshire, so they made him their mascot and named him Derby.

No regiment ever had a more faithful pet. He marched three thousand miles with the Foresters and followed them into six battles, where they fought as bravely as Robin Hood's men in Sherwood Forest, from which their name came. Derby always guarded the camp and showed a fighting spirit as strong as his regiment's. If a thief or another male sheep came near, Derby would lower his great curved horns, charge and deliver a terrific butt. He hit like a battering-ram, the log with a bronze ram's head on its end which the Romans used to batter down the gates of enemy cities.

After the rebellion was quelled, Derby, along with other veterans, was decorated with the Indian medal. It was pinned on a beautiful scarlet coat, made for him by wives of officers of his regiment. That was his dress uniform, and he looked proud when he wore it. What a splendid sight he was as he marched in front of the band at parades, a plume nodding between his horns and a silver bell tinkling at his neck!

In 1863 Derby fell into a well and drowned, but he was never forgotten, for he had founded a long line of mascot rams, all named Derby and dressed and decorated exactly as he had been.

Derby II and III joined the regiment in India and returned with the Foresters to England. On the ship going home the rams were part of a regular zoo the troops had collected. It made the ship look like Noah's Ark. There was a bear, a panther, an Indian antelope called a nilgai, a huge boa constrictor and about a thousand chattering parakeets. But the two rams were kings of the zoo because they were the official mascots.

Each of the Derby rams had different ways and likes and dislikes, but all of them were rambunctious. Derby I had been fond of music and musicians, especially bass drummers. Another Derby was just the opposite and had to be held tightly during parades because the sound of horns and drums made him wild. Once he broke loose, charged the band and strewed the drill ground with butted bandsmen and battered instruments. Derby VIII behaved well at weekday parades, but he objected

57

to the solemn music the band played on Sunday, and refused to march to church.

That eighth Derby had joined the regiment with his brother. The Foresters could not decide at first which would be Derby VIII and which Derby IX, but finally they chose the one that liked lively music as the handsomer of the two. The rejected brother was wildly jealous and flew into such tantrums that he had to be sent back to civilian life.

Derby XV was an Indian ram, the gift of the Maharajah of Kotah, home of the first mascot. Natives called him "The Sacred Sheep," but he acted less and less holy as he grew older. One night he woke up in a bad humor and went on a ripsnorting rampage through the barracks. An enemy attack could scarcely have caused more terrific confusion. Sleeping soldiers were butted out of their bunks and routed by those big curved horns. Derby turned from chasing them to raid the quarters of the Commanding Officer's native servants, who escaped his charges only by climbing trees. When the ram was worn out by his sport he quieted down, but needless to say he was confined the next day to a strongly fenced pasture.

To take his place, Derby XVI, a present to the Foresters from the Duke of Devonshire, was shipped from England. The woolly youngster gave the ram-orderlies, who met him at the dock, such a lively tussle that they had a hard time leading him to camp. Trouble was expected between the new mascot and the old one, but they never quarreled. Derby XV watched the young ram's training with keen interest, and seemed to understand that the sooner the recruit learned to march in parades, the sooner he, the veteran, could retire. Both rams eventually went back to England with the regiment, and there the old Derby was put out to pasture and Derby XVI took over his duties.

Derby XVII serves with the Sherwood Foresters today. When he marches, the silver bell worn by Derby I tinkles at his neck. And that same bell is still rung before dinner in the officers' mess in memory of the original ram that became a famous mascot instead of mutton chops.

Sam

NEWFOUNDLAND OF THE ROYAL CANADIANS

THE PUPPY was born to be a fisherman's dog. Fishermen had brought his breed from Europe to help them in their work on the coasts of Newfoundland, and the dogs were named after that Canadian province. When this puppy with jet-black curly hair grew up into a big, powerful dog weighing one hundred and fifty pounds, he would be taught how to grasp a net, loaded with fish, in his teeth and tug away alongside men hauling it in to the beach. Also he would be able to carry a pack, or pull a cart or sled. His webbed feet would make him a wonderful swimmer, and his thick coat would protect him so well in icy waters that he could save drowning people or carry a life line through the surf to a sinking ship.

But the puppy turned out to be a soldier's dog. An English lieutenant stationed in Canada bought him in 1858 and named him Sam. When the officer was later ordered home, he took Sam, now grown into a large dog, aboard the transport with him. His pet would be happy in England, where Newfoundlands had become as great favorites as they were in America.

On the same ship was a new regiment, the Royal Canadians, later known as The Prince of Wales's Leinster Regiment. Canada had recruited it and was sending it across the ocean to reinforce the British army, which had suffered heavy losses in the Crimean War and the Indian Mutiny. Sam strolled around the crowded decks and made many friends by his gentle, endearing ways. When the transport reached England, Sam's master called him to go ashore, but Sam lay down and wouldn't budge. He was no longer a one-man dog—his heart belonged to a whole regiment. Finally the lieutenant sighed and gave up. He presented the Newfoundland to the patriotic troops who had come to help England in her hour of need.

Sam marched with the Royal Canadians to the training camp at Aldershot—straight into plenty of trouble. No dogs were allowed there. The military police, under orders to catch and destroy all dogs found in camp, arrested Sam and shut him up in the guardhouse.

Word that Sam was a prisoner, condemned to death, spread like wildfire among the Royal Canadians. A crowd of angry soldiers gathered and rushed shouting to the rescue of their pet. With flying fists they pitched into the M.P.'s. It was a knockdown and drag-out fight that made Aldershot's war maneuvers look like a parlor game. Sam heard the din of battle and barked savagely, trying to break out of his prison and join his friends in combat. It was lucky for his captors that the big Newfoundland could not win free to spring at their throats. The fighting-mad Canadians, managing without him, released Sam and led him back to barracks. Bruised and battered police picked themselves up and made a report that caused the Colonel of the Canadians to be summoned to Headquarters before the Commanding Officer.

The Colonel explained that he and his regiment had not known about the regulation against dogs. It might be necessary, he admitted, to dispose of stray dogs, which otherwise would overrun the camp. But Sam was a regular mascot that marched in front of the band at parades, and all the regiment loved him. "If any further attempt is made to destroy our mascot," the Colonel finished, "I cannot be responsible, sir, for what my men may do."

Those were bold words to a superior, but it happened that the Commanding Officer liked dogs and understood how the Canadians felt. He granted permission for Sam to stay in camp, but only on condition that he be kept tied up and not allowed to roam. So Sam was shut up in a stable and tethered by a strong rope.

When the Canadians marched off one day to a Divisional review, the Newfoundland stayed quiet until he heard the blare of their band in the distance. That was more than he could bear; he belonged at its head. Whining, he jerked at his rope, then gnawed through it and broke down the door. Out he dashed to follow the trail of his friends for several miles down Long Valley till he lost it among many footprints. Head up, he raced on. Troops drawn up on Long Common saw a black streak speeding toward them. Sam, trailing a yard of rope, trotted along the front of three full brigades in line. The drill was held up, and noncoms snapped at privates in the ranks to wipe those silly grins off their faces.

At last Sam uttered a short, joyous bark. There they were—

his own Royal Canadians in their uniforms of scarlet with blue facings. He ran up and took his usual place in front of the band. Never afterward was it denied him.

The mascot served with his regiment when it was sent to Gibraltar, and later to the Mediterranean island of Malta. He drew beef rations from the quartermaster for breakfast, lunched with the sergeants and had dinner at the officers' mess. But he never became fat and lazy, or neglected his duties of standing guard, parading and going on all maneuvers.

On the target range at Malta he forgot to keep under cover, and a bullet severely wounded him in the neck. Although he recovered and accompanied the Canadians when they were ordered back to their homeland in 1866, the cold of a bitter winter affected his wound, which had never entirely healed, and he died.

As a memorial to Sam, his beautiful black coat was tanned and made into an apron for the bass drummer of the band he had loved to lead at parades.

Old Abe

EAGLE OF THE 8TH WISCONSIN

TWO EAGLETS sat snug in their nest at the top of a tall Wisconsin pine, one spring day in 1861. High in the air, they seemed safe from harm, but the keen eyes of a Chippewa Indian spotted them.

It would be a hard and dangerous feat to climb that big tree and rob the nest. Instead, the Indian swung his ax with sturdy blows that made the sharp blade bite deep into the tree trunk. The pine swayed, toppled and crashed to the ground. As the Indian ran toward the fallen nest and its eaglets, their angry parents flew over and swooped down to the rescue of their young. Savagely the Chippewa beat them off until they gave up and winged, screeching, away.

One of the eaglets had been killed by the fall, but his brother was unhurt. When the Indian reached for him he fought fiercely, young though he was, and it cost his captor a struggle to thrust him into a sack.

American eagles, hard to catch, could usually be sold or traded. The Indian swapped his prize for a bushel of corn. Twice more the eaglet changed hands. His third owner made a present of him to the 8th Wisconsin Regiment, which had enlisted to fight in the Civil War. They made the eaglet their mascot and named him Old Abe after President Abraham Lincoln.

Old Abe soon grew to be a magnificent bird with fine brown feathers and a crest of snowy white. His fierce hooked beak and curved talons were as sharp as they looked, and he used them on anyone who teased him, though he was tame if he was not annoyed. To keep him from flying away, a leather band was fastened to one of his legs, and attached to the band was a thong which tethered him to his perch. The thong was twenty feet long and let him soar that far aloft.

The 8th Regiment was proud of Old Abe. Other Wisconsin troops had badgers, the state animal, as their mascots, and one drummer boy owned a squirrel that would race around the rim of his master's drum when the roll was beaten. But the 8th thought that its eagle, the national bird, was the finest mascot in the whole Union Army.

When the 8th marched, its fifes shrilling "Yankee Doodle" and drums rattling, Old Abe was carried on his perch by the eagle-bearer at the left of the Stars and Stripes. Spectators cheered and clapped their hands, and Old Abe responded by spreading and flapping his wings. Then the eagle would reach down and take the corner of a small American flag, tied to his perch, in his beak, and the crowds would go wild with enthusiasm.

Guns thundered, and Old Abe went into action with the 8th, first at the capture of Island Number 10 in the Mississippi, then at New Madrid and Farmington. No longer could his regiment doubt that he would behave in battle as an American eagle should. When shells burst and muskets cracked, Old Abe spread his wings and screamed defiance. What a stirring spectacle it made—that Blue line charging, with Old Glory and Old Abe in its center, their brave bearers slanting them forward against the steel blast from the Gray trenches!

On the march, Old Abe learned to drink from a canteen; he'd tilt back his head and open his beak for his bearer to pour water down his throat. When the beef ration ran out, his soldier friends foraged rabbits, squirrels and poultry for him. Sometimes he fished for minnows, of which he was fond, and he liked to bathe in creeks. When the 8th was in camp in Mississippi he was given liberty, and flew around on visits to the entire brigade, always returning to C Company at night. Sometimes he fell into temporary disgrace because he tore up laundry drying on lines or stole chickens from the cook.

But when the bugles blew, he was eager and ready at his post. His fame spread throughout the Army of the West. When Generals Grant and Sherman met the 8th Wisconsin, they lifted their hats to Old Abe.

Corinth was Old Abe's greatest battle. There was a rumor that the Confederates were determined to capture "that Yankee buzzard," but the eagle, hackles high with excitement, was carried forward with the skirmish line as usual. When the enemy's artillery fire grew heavy, and the men of the 8th were ordered to take cover, Old Abe hopped down from his perch and flattened himself on the ground too. But when the Gray infantry charged with a shrill Rebel yell, the eagle was up again as fast as men of the 8th. From his perch he watched a volley blaze from the

Blue line and saw the Confederate ranks stagger back, but they valiantly attacked again, pouring in a hail of lead. Two musket balls ripped through Eagle-bearer McLain's uniform, while a third bullet cut the hemp cord that tied Old Abe to his perch. The American eagle soared, screaming, above the battle line, as shells from a Yankee battery shattered the Confederate assault.

After the battle, a Wisconsin soldier told a tall story with a grin. He boasted that he had seen Old Abe clutch two rocks from a stone fence with his talons and fly over and drop them on the heads of the enemy.

Altogether Old Abe saw action in thirty-six battles and skirmishes. It was considered an honor to carry him, just as it was an honor to carry the flag, and he had six different bearers, who had to be strong men because the eagle weighed fourteen pounds. None of the bearers was killed, though they and the eagle made easy targets and were often under heavy fire.

After three years of service Old Abe retired to a room reserved for him in the Wisconsin State Capitol, with his private perch in its park. No reunion, either of his own regiment or of any other in the state, was complete without him, and he usually recognized his fellow veterans, especially his bearers, and screeched a greeting when they met. He went to rallies to help elect General Grant President of the United States, and listened politely to a speech by General Sherman, but he ruffled his feathers when that officer, no Wisconsin man, tried to pet him. For years he traveled around the country to raise money for worthy causes; sales of his molted feathers at five dollars each and of his photographs brought in $80,000. As late as the First

World War, pictures of him were being sold for the benefit of the Red Cross. Poems and six books were written about him, and he posed for two marble sculptures.

Once the eagle was neglected by a careless attendant and nearly died, but he was rescued and afterward he was always given the good care he deserved. In 1880 he survived a fire that burned the Capitol, but he never recovered from the fumes. The following year Old Abe, the war eagle, who had flapped his mighty wings in the smoke of battle, died, and millions of Americans mourned for him.

Stonewall

THE RICHMOND HOWITZERS' DOG

ONE DAY in the second year of the Civil War, a small dog, white with jet-black spots, trotted up to the men of a Confederate artillery regiment in position near Richmond, Virginia. Cannoneers stooped down and patted him. The dog wagged his tail to show he wanted to stay with these soldiers in gray.

He had made a good choice, for he was such a little fellow that he couldn't have kept up with infantry making long marches. With the men of the horse-drawn artillery, the Richmond Howitzers, the dog could ride on one of the gun carriages.

The Howitzers welcomed him as a mascot and named him Stonewall after the great Confederate General, "Stonewall" Jackson. Every man in the regiment was a friend of the lively, playful dog, but his special favorite was Sergeant Van, chief of a gun crew.

Sergeant Van taught his pet to sit up on his haunches at roll call. The sergeant had carved a small pipe which Stonewall carried clamped in his jaws until the command "Pipes out" was given. Then Van would bend down, take the pipe from the dog's mouth and put it between the toes of his left forepaw. Stonewall would lower the pipe to his side and sit at attention, as straight and stiff as any man in the ranks.

A second mascot, a larger dog named Bobby Lee, joined the Richmond Howitzers about the same time that Stonewall did. Bobby was brave in fights with dogs of other regiments, fights which Stonewall kept away from because he was so small. As his artillery friends said, "He didn't carry enough guns."

But the behavior of the two dogs was exactly the opposite when the Howitzers went into battle against Union troops. Bobby, frightened by the firing, would run away and hide, trembling, behind a tree. After the shooting stopped he would creep back, looking ashamed. Stonewall, though, acted like a regular dog of war. He capered around among the thundering guns, leaping up and down as if to encourage the cannoneers to fire faster. In one of those sudden silences which sometimes

happen in the midst of a battle, the men could hear his shrill barks.

When horses brought up limbers to move the battery, one of the artillerymen would pick up Stonewall and drop him into an empty compartment of an ammunition chest. Off galloped the teams to a new position. As soon as the guns were unlimbered to begin fire again, Stonewall was lifted out to dash about and yip encouragement to the busy cannoneers.

Stonewall's antics kept spirits high at the fierce Battle of Chancellorsville. The Richmond Howitzers had placed their guns in a flower bed. Yankee batteries found their range, and

such a storm of shells burst over the Confederate artillerymen that many of them were hit and the flowers were dyed red with their blood. But they would not desert their flaming cannon, and their gallant little mascot never left them for an instant. When the Yankees fell back in defeat, Stonewall, unwounded and as lively as ever, chimed in with high-pitched barks as his comrades cheered the victory.

The fame Stonewall won by his courage and clever tricks spread to other regiments, who were envious of the Howitzers with their spunky mascot. When Stonewall disappeared, his anxious masters went searching for him through the camps of troops near them. At last they found him tied to a tent pole in the encampment of a Louisiana brigade, with soldiers feeding and petting him. Then and there a private war almost started inside the Confederate army. The Howitzers accused the Louisianans of stealing their dog. Nothing of the sort, snapped back the men from the Deep South—they were only being kind to a stray that wandered into their area and looked hungry. Before a fight could begin, Stonewall proved whose dog he was by showing how glad he was to see the Howitzers. He almost pulled the tent pole down trying to reach them. The Louisianans had to give him up, and the Howitzers took their mascot back in triumph to the artillery lines.

Once more Stonewall vanished. His masters hunted for him everywhere, but this time in vain. He must have been too well hidden, the Howitzers said bitterly.

Their mascot was lost to the regiment for the rest of the war, but he belongs to them in history. For Major Robert Stiles, who wrote a fine book about the service of the Richmond Howitzers, made Stonewall the hero of one of its chapters.

74

Bobby

BOBBY, born in Malta, was a rough-and-ready rough-haired terrier, white except for brownish ears. He wandered around that Mediterranean island as a stray dog, living on scraps, until he made friends with some soldiers. They were the Royal Berkshires, part of the island's British garrison, and they gave Bobby a warm welcome. He would make a fine mascot, they thought, because he was small and could be smuggled out of the sight of inspectors who might be fussy about dogs with the army. Also he was sturdy enough for long marches and he was a cocky fighter.

So Bobby became the Berkshires' pet, and they took him along when they were sent to Afghanistan in Asia to help put down an uprising of fierce and warlike tribes rebelling against the British.

The Berkshires joined a force of 2300 men under General Burrows—Indian infantry and cavalry, and British batteries of artillery—mustered at the town of Kandahar. When the column marched out against the rebels in the hot summer of 1880,

75

Bobby took his place in the ranks of the Berkshires. Although the terrier suffered as greatly as the men from the blistering July heat, and the rocky ground hurt his paws, he did not straggle. He was close beside his friends when the Afghans, under their ablest chieftain, Ayoub Khan, swept down to attack near the village of Maiwand.

The tribesmen, savage and deadly warriors armed with rifles and long curved swords, were ten to one against the British, who reeled back before the fury of an onslaught by overwhelming numbers. But the Berkshires rallied and stood firm, firing steady volleys, and Bobby stayed with them. In the dreadful confusion of the battle, some dogs might have put their tails between their legs and run. Not Bobby—he would not leave his comrades.

A wild, whooping charge by the Afghan cavalry broke the Indian troops and scattered them in panic-stricken rout. Then the Berkshires formed the famous British square, a fort with walls of men. Volleys blazed and bayonets bristled along its four sides. Inside the square Bobby raced from wall to wall, barking encouragement as his soldiers drove off the turbaned horsemen.

But when the Berkshires broke their formation to march off and cover the retreat of the rest of the army, they could not hold back the enemy. Their Colonel was killed saving the colors, and their companies were split apart and scattered. For a time one hundred of the survivors defended a walled garden. Then howling Afghan warriors flooded over it, and only one officer and ten riflemen lived to fight their way out. At their heels ran a small white terrier.

Three hundred yards away they made a last stand, back to back. From a distance their comrades, fighting so desperately for their own lives that they could not come to the rescue, saw the eleven blazing away with rifles and revolvers. In front of them stood Bobby, teeth bared and barking defiance.

When the enemy closed in, Bobby bit them savagely. He would not leave until the last of the eleven fell. Then he rushed forward, growling and snapping, and the Afghans jumped out of his path. The running dog disappeared in the cloud of dust covering the battlefield.

Remaining companies of the Berkshires, struggling miles back toward their base over the burning desert, were sure they had seen the last of their mascot. But when relief troops from Kandahar met them, a soldier looked to the rear and sighted a small white speck. Bobby, bloody and dust-caked, limped up on raw paws, his back gashed by a long bullet furrow.

Bobby's wound healed, and he finished the campaign, which the British army finally won. Back to England he sailed with the Berkshires, and there a great day awaited them and him.

Queen Victoria summoned officers and men of the Battalion to be thanked for their gallant conduct at Maiwand, and of course they took their mascot along, since the Queen had asked especially for him. After Her Majesty had presented new colors to the Berkshires, Bobby was led up. He was wearing a scarlet coat to cover the long scar on his back, and the Queen asked that it be taken off so that she could see the mark of the wound he had suffered in her service. For several moments she looked down tenderly at the brave little terrier, and his bright eyes gazed up at her. Then Victoria bent, smiling, to pat Bobby's

white head and to fasten to his collar the medal of the Second Afghan War.

Bobby, like so many other mascots who lived through battles, died in a peacetime accident. A cab with a runaway horse hit and killed him.

His stuffed hide is kept in the museum of the Royal Berkshires. There, too, hangs an oil painting by Frank Fuller, an artist of the Royal Academy—a painting called "The Last Eleven at Maiwand." It shows those valiant soldiers fighting to the end, and with them their brave and faithful companion, Bobby.

Wahb

U.S. INFANTRY BEAR

ADVENTURES CAME early and fast to the bear cub. Soon after he was born in the jungles of Borneo, in far eastern Asia, hunters captured him and presented him to a native prince. Next came a voyage across the Sulu Sea in a small sailing vessel, carrying the cub and his royal owner to the southern islands of the Philippines, where the fierce Moro tribes lived.

There were new rulers over the Philippines in that year of 1899. The United States had just won the islands from Spain in a war, and the villages were garrisoned by tall soldiers in khaki whom the Moros liked better than they had the Spaniards. The Borneo prince, eager to get on well with the Americans, made a gift of the bear cub to Lieutenant Colonel Sydney A. Cloman of the 23rd Infantry.

Colonel Cloman found that the wild little bundle of black fur was a handful of trouble—mostly teeth, claws and deviltry. But Wahb, as the cub was named, grew tame when he was treated kindly and given all the coconut juice and condensed milk he could drink. His antics were wonderful entertainment for the lonely, homesick infantrymen.

They never tired of watching the bear and an old monkey

named Jane. She would put her arms around him and try to mother him. The cub decided he was too old for that sort of thing. He'd lift a small paw and cuff her, Jane would bite him, and a fight would rage through the house. Yet soon they would make up their quarrel, and Wahb would let the monkey ride around on his back.

Another amusing show was the boxing and wrestling bouts which Wahb and General Kobbe's fox terrier often staged. Growling loudly, they would wallop away at each other with their paws, or roll over and over, tangled up together, upsetting the bamboo furniture and rumpling the matting. It was all in good fun, and neither of them ever lost his temper. Though the bear sometimes took the dog's whole head in his mouth, he was careful never to hurt his friend.

Wahb delighted in his daily bath and in walks with Colonel Cloman. The bear would run on ahead, then wait and look back, exactly like a dog that wants its master to hurry. In the evening he would curl up on a cushion at the Colonel's feet. If he heard a noise outside he would wake and snarl a warning. No watchdog could have done a better job.

Natives had warned Colonel Cloman that Borneo bears, even though they have been tamed as cubs, may turn savage when they grow older. The officer doubted the story, but one day it suddenly came true. Wahb howled and charged his master. The Colonel had to defend himself with a baseball bat he snatched up, or be badly bitten and clawed. A couple of sharp raps on Wahb's thick skull convinced him that life as a wild animal was not as pleasant as being a pet. He never forgot his lesson, and always afterward he and his master were devoted friends.

But Wahb's good behavior ended whenever he smelled chop suey cooking in a Chinese restaurant. Into the shack he would dash. It would echo with wild confusion, as dishes crashed, and pots and pans clattered. Diners yelled and scrambled out the windows. The cook popped out the back door like a cork out of a bottle and dashed madly into the jungle. After Wahb had eaten all the chop suey in the place and anything else he fancied, he would stroll out, licking his jaws and looking highly pleased with himself. Then Colonel Cloman would have to pay the bill for lost dinners and damages.

One time Wahb caused trouble that was not really his fault at all. General Kobbe saw the bear ambling peacefully along the village street. Quickly Kobbe hid behind a hut, and when the mascot approached he jumped out and shouted, "Boo!"

The next thing the General knew he was running for his life, with the furious animal hot after him. Although Borneo bears are not large, their teeth and claws are sharp, and the General didn't care to feel Wahb's. Moros stared unbelievingly at the Commanding Officer sprinting at top speed, the angry bear snapping at his heels. In the nick of time Colonel Cloman came to the rescue and managed to catch Wahb and chain him up.

"I'll never try to scare another bear as long as I live!" gasped General Kobbe, panting for breath.

After three years in the Philippines, Colonel Cloman was ordered home and he planned to take Wahb with him. That would not be allowed, he was told. There was a ruling against taking animals, which might carry disease, from Asia to the United States. But the Colonel would not give up, and he was supported by General Kobbe and even by the Governor of the Philippines. Finally permission was granted on condition that the bear be given to the National Zoo in Washington. Colonel Cloman agreed, since he could visit his mascot at the zoo.

Wahb proudly followed his master aboard a gunboat and became the favorite of all hands. But during the voyage he grew thirsty one day and saw a bucket full of green liquid that looked like something good to drink. Unfortunately it was paint, poisonous because of the lead that was mixed with it. The bear gulped it down. In spite of all that could be done to save his life, Wahb died.

Colonel Colman had become so fond of Wahb that he would never own another pet. When he wrote a book about his service in the land of the Moros, the little Borneo bear was his happiest memory.

Percy

CHIMPANZEE OF THE GOLD COAST REGIMENT

A MOTHER CHIMPANZEE and her son, walking through an African forest, never saw the native hunter who raised his musket and fired. The mother monkey was killed, and when the little one tried to escape, the hunter caught him and tied him up, but only at the cost of a badly bitten finger. Then the captor carried his prize to the British station at West Ashanti and sold him to the Commissioner for five shillings.

Percy, as the baby monkey was named, was motherless, but the Commissioner treated him as a kind father would, and all the British officers at the post appointed themselves his "uncles." Very soon he began to brighten life for everybody in that dull and lonely place. Percy was a whole circus in himself and got into every sort of mischief. He spilled ink, chewed erasers and played with matches until he burned his whiskers. He would dive from the veranda and roll in the Commissioner's best zinnia bed, but he left the roses alone after one painful experience with their thorns. The garden had to be fenced to save bananas and tomatoes from his raids. Percy collected new-laid eggs as a between-meals snack, and he was broken of that habit only by an angry hen who chased him and gave him a good pecking. When new phonograph records arrived from England, Percy clashed them together like cymbals. Although he was scolded for his naughtiness and corrected, he was praised for such brave deeds as killing a snake in the bathroom and hauling out a poisonous tarantula that had crept into one of his master's boots.

Each evening before dinner Percy joined the officers for drinks, and demanded a lime-juice cocktail. At table he sat on a high chair next to the president of the mess, and handled his spoon and glass nicely. His table manners were good except for splashing when he served himself with fruit salad, his favorite dish, or when he stole a tidbit from somebody else's plate. After dinner he would entertain by dancing a jig to the tune of "Pop Goes the Weasel," marching to bagpipe music and doing acrobatic feats on the chandelier. At bedtime he insisted on kissing his master and all his "uncles" good night.

A bull terrier that once nipped Percy in the leg never dared do it again. The chimp, uttering his war cry of "Wuffoo," picked up a stick and drove his enemy around and around the garden until the yipping dog plunged into a water tank. But Percy held nothing against dogs in general, and in fact adopted a puppy, which was devoted to him even though he carried it around hugged upside down in his arms, or dragged it by the tail. Finally the pup ran away to find an easier life than that of being Percy's pet.

Whenever the Commissioner held court, Percy presided with him on the bench, and he always accompanied his owner on inspection trips. Once, as they approached a village, drummers were heard beating a message, and the Commissioner asked his clerk what the drums said. "Master," the man answered, "they say fine monkey coming and bringing Commissioner."

The chimpanzee was one year old when the Commissioner, going home on leave and not able to take him, consented to Percy's joining the army. All the companies of the Gold Coast Regiment asked for him, but it was the Pioneer and Engineer Company that won the honor of his thumb-mark on its muster

roll. The chimpanzee soldier was given an orderly of his own who dressed him every morning in his specially tailored uniform exactly like that of the native troops—a red zouave jacket with sash, khaki shorts, and a red fez with a black tassel, cocked at a rakish angle on his head. Percy fenced cleverly with a stick held like a sword, and smoked a pipe like a veteran, but drill bored him, and he spent most of his time sampling food in the kitchens or pounding nails in the carpenter shop. He upset the dignity of inspections by his custom of kissing the Colonel.

Doing some inspecting of his own one day, the chimpanzee found a box of high-explosive fuses in a rack and was pulling them down when the color sergeant spotted him and yelled to his captain:

"Hop it, sir, quick! Percy's at the detonators!"

The two men ran for their lives, with Percy after them, dragging the box and chewing on one of the fuses. Before he could blow himself up and his friends, too, his orderly snatched the chimp's dangerous toys away from him.

Though Percy had shown he wasn't afraid to "monkey" with explosives, he did not campaign with his regiment against the Germans in Africa when the First World War broke out. His master, the Commissioner, had returned, and Percy was mustered out of the army to rejoin him. Officers of the regiment gave a dinner for their mascot—a great success, though Percy accidentally put his foot in the Colonel's soup—and next morning bugles blew him a farewell.

Later on Percy was taken to England, where he settled down in a zoo. He would have been lonely there if Colonel B. V. Ramsden and other old friends had not occasionally stopped in for a visit and to smoke a pipe with him as they used to in Africa. In 1918, after the shock of an air raid, the clever, affectionate chimpanzee died of penumonia, leaving behind him many endearing memories.

Bella and Bertha

COWS OF THE SCOTS GUARDS

"THE GERMANS are coming!"

That dreaded alarm spread through the French village of
Fourbaix in the first winter of World War I. Terrified people
hitched horses to farm wagons, loaded what belongings they
could into them and perched grandparents and little children
on top. Then they hurried away from the enemy in such haste
that they had to leave cows and chickens behind. Soon the
abandoned cows began lowing pitifully to be fed and milked,
and the chickens vainly scratched at the hard ground for worms.

But the Germans never came after all. The troops of Kaiser
Wilhelm II, a dark tide in field-gray uniforms which had been
about to flow over Fourbaix and flood all of France, ebbed back
in retreat before an advancing British army. First to enter the
deserted village was the 2nd Battalion of the Scots Guards, trim
in Glengarry caps, khaki tunics and kilts. The Germans never
cared to meet Scots, whose kilts and fierce fighting had won
them the name of "Ladies from Hell."

The Scotsmen, who had not tasted fresh meat for two weeks,
eyed the cattle and the poultry hungrily but would not touch

the property of their allies, the French. Yet the cows and fowl would starve before the villagers could return. Something had to be done. The Battalion Quartermaster found an answer: buy the cattle and poultry, send the money to their owners and serve up a fine beef-and-chicken dinner.

Butchers and cooks, preparing for a feast, hesitated to slaughter two of the cows. Both animals were especially thin and scrawny, and there was an appealing look in their soft brown eyes. Soldiers gathered around to pat them and murmur "Puir coos!" sympathetically in their Scots burr. They couldn't bear to let those two be killed.

Instead they made the cows their mascots and named them Bella and Bertha. A soldier who used to work on a farm was put in charge of them and was laughingly called the "Coo Major" by all the Battalion. But he knew his job, and herded the cows on with the Guards when they marched forward again.

Bella and Bertha, well fed now, grew fat and healthy, and filled many a pail brimful of milk for their friends. The walking dairies kept their place in the rear of the column and never straggled. But marches were long, and soon their hoofs began to wear down. It was plain that they couldn't go much farther.

Sadness spread through the Battalion. Every Guardsman hated the thought of leaving the mascots behind. The cows could be turned over to some farmer who would take good care of them, but then the Scots would probably never see them again. If Bella and Bertha had been horses, the answer would have been easy: "Shoe them." But cows are cloven-footed with a split in each hoof—not solid-hoofed like horses. At last a blacksmith in the Battalion offered to try to shoe the cows. He hammered out double "coo shoes" on an anvil and nailed them on, and they worked perfectly. Bella and Bertha stepped out proudly and tirelessly over the hard white French roads.

Other troops, seldom able to buy milk from farms, envied the Scots—lucky Jocks, as they called them, with a couple of dairies on the hoof to give them cream in their tea and maybe butter and cheese if there was a churn handy. Every Guardsman took his turn and had his share of milk.

Bella and Bertha, besides being good milkers, were great pets. They proved they were regular mascots when Pipe-Major Mac-Intosh signaled his band. Drums thudded and the bagpipes skirled, playing the regimental march "Highland Laddie." The

two cows lifted their heads and waggled their horns. Then they trotted forward to be closer to the music. There wasn't a doubt they loved the pipes as much as any Scotsman.

During the campaign in Belgium, Bella and Bertha each presented the Battalion with a calf. One died, but the other lived and was sent as a gift to Princess Mary.

In spite of shot and shell, the two cows served with the Scots Guards through all four years of the war. When it ended they were taken to London to march in the Victory Parade, as such faithful companions and fellow veterans well deserved. Their hides were brushed sleek. Handsome browbands of red and white were put on them, and their horns were painted the colors

of the Stuart tartan, which their regiment has the right to wear. Once more Bella and Bertha took their place in ranks and heard the familiar order to march and the stirring music of their beloved bagpipes. Yonder the colors fluttered brightly, colors that had been furled and cased in wartime.

This was a special occasion, the cows must have sensed, as animals do. Their soldier friends had fussed over them, making them handsome for this review. Never had they stepped out more proudly. As the column passed before King George V the command "Eyes left" was given. Thousands saw Bella and Bertha turn their heads and obey the order as smartly as any Guardsman.

For a time Bella and Bertha were put to graze in Hyde Park, where they became the most popular sight of London, admired by the public and praised by the newspapers. Later they were given a home on the estate of a nobleman in Scotland, where they ended their lives, full of years and honor. Silver statuettes of them were made, and snuffboxes were carved from one hoof of each. Those tokens will always be kept by the Scots Guards in memory of their famous mascot cows.

Prince

TERRIER OF THE NORTH STAFFORDSHIRES

WHILE Private James Brown was stationed in Ireland with the North Staffordshire regiment of the British army before the First World War, he bought a strong Irish terrier and named him Prince. The dog's love and loyalty were for his master first, but his heart was warm for the rest of the regiment too. Every day he made the rounds of the barracks visiting friends, and often spent the night with them. He had learned that if he went home his master's wife might insist on giving him one of those baths he hated.

Prince never missed a march, and usually he traveled two miles for every one the column covered. Often there were impudent rabbits to be chased; though he never caught one, he ran them into their burrows and, trying to dig them out, made the dirt fly faster than the Staffordshires when they dug trenches. When Prince sighted other dogs along the route, he treated them as enemy scouts and attacked. He pitched into them no matter how big they were, and routed them, yelping, by the fury of his charge. Prince's comrades cheered him. "He's a stout fellow," they said, "and whatever danger he meets, he never lowers his tail."

The terrier had been training with his regiment for two years when the First World War began and the North Staffordshires were ordered to France. From the way Prince hung around the men's kits and their packed equipment it was plain that he expected to go along. All ranks wanted to take him, but at last they made the hard decision to leave him behind. As soldiers, they must take their chances in battle, but it didn't seem fair to risk Prince's life.

Just before the regiment broke camp, the dog was shut up by Private Brown's wife in her cottage. He was afraid he was going to be given another of those hateful baths, but it was worse than that. Before long he came to understand that he had been deserted by the men he loved.

Soon afterward Mrs. Brown moved with Prince to London. From a window of a little house in the big city the lonely dog kept vain watch for his soldier friends. Then one day he saw another regiment, the Queen's Westminsters, marching down the street on their way to embark for France. They wore the same uniform as the North Staffordshires, and Prince dashed out and trotted after them.

When Mrs. Brown missed him she searched the neighborhood and advertised in the newspapers, but Prince couldn't be found. At last she sadly wrote her husband that his pet and the regiment's favorite had disappeared.

Prince quickly discovered that the troops he had joined were not his own. He had gone sniffing through the ranks, but nobody smelled familiar. Still, it was good to be with soldiers again, and these were kind fellows who welcomed the friendly terrier. Prince followed them aboard the boat that took them across the Channel to France. At his old tireless trot he marched beside them to the front, where they were to take over trenches in the Armentières sector.

Prince was a lucky dog. Out of half a million British troops in France, the very first regiment the Westminsters met when they moved up into the line under German gunfire was the North Staffordshires.

For a moment Prince stood stiffly, looking and sniffing. Then there was a sudden outburst of joyful barking and a flash of brown hide. Private Brown was nearly knocked over by the rush of a quivering body and fond forepaws violently planted on his chest. Prince had found his beloved master.

The wonderful news that the lost mascot had rejoined spread through the regiment as fast as the frantic wagging of the terrier's tail. Brown, ordered to report to the Commanding Officer with his pet, had a hard time reaching headquarters through crowds of men who wanted to pat Prince. The Colonel made as much fuss over him as everybody else, while Private Brown stood at stiff attention, grinning happily.

Prince went right back on duty. Every night he went forward with ammunition and ration details to visit the front-line trenches and dugouts. As stout a fellow as ever, he never hesitated at crossroads where shells were bursting, or on bullet-swept trails. His friends were waiting for him, and he had affection and companionship to give them. Bearers carrying a

95

wounded man back to a dressing station would halt to let Prince put his paws up on the litter, show the sympathy in his eloquent brown eyes and lick a cold hand stretched out to pat him.

One evening a shell fragment gave Prince a wound of his own. A sergeant bandaged him as best he could and tied him in a shelter to keep him quiet. But Prince refused to stay on the sick list for long. He whined and struggled so that it seemed wise to let him out. With his wound only half healed, he went back to the front to see his friends, who had been missing him as much as he had them.

The brave terrier carried on through all four years of the war. He was growing old and worn out from all the hardships he'd endured, but he stood by his regiment till the end. When the Armistice was signed and the North Staffordshires marched through France on their way home, Prince trotted beside them, ears perked and tail as high as ever.

Prince served on through several years of peace with his master and other comrades. Then the gallant mascot, whom German barrages and bullets could not kill, somehow found and ate a scrap of poisoned meat. Veterinaries tried hard, but they couldn't save him.

Today Prince's picture hangs in the North Staffordshires' museum. "There is no tombstone to mark the place where his body lies," a major of the regiment wrote, "and none is necessary, for his life is deeply engraven on the hearts of those who knew him."

Whiskey and Soda

LIONS OF THE LAFAYETTE ESCADRILLE

ABOARD a French ship bound homeward from Africa, a lioness gave birth to a lusty male cub. When the ship docked, the mother was sent to a zoo, and the son was given to a Brazilian dentist living in Paris. His owner fed the cub by dipping his finger in milk and letting the little animal suck it, but soon the lion's baby teeth grew sharp. Dentists don't like to be bitten by either pets or patients, so the cub was put up for sale.

The First World War was on, and nobody seemed to want to buy a lion. Then officers of the Lafayette Escadrille came to town on leave from the front. That dashing, hard-fighting squadron of French army fliers included Lieutenants Raoul Lufberry, William K. Thaw, Norman Hall and other Americans.

When they heard about the lion for sale, they said, "A lion is lucky, and we can get this one cheap." Gladly they chipped in 125 francs, bought the cub as their mascot and named him Whiskey.

There was trouble when the mascot was carried aboard a train to be taken to the Escadrille's flying field. His escort, Lieutenant Thaw, had bought a ticket for a dog, but the conductor looked at Whiskey and demanded suspiciously, "What is that animal there?"

"An African dog," Thaw answered, keeping his face straight.

Whiskey gave himself away. He opened his mouth wide and took a deep breath. What came out of his throat was no bark. It was a small but unmistakable roar.

"But it's a lion!" the conductor exclaimed. Two women passengers who had been petting the "African dog" screamed and ran down the corridor of the car. The cub was put off the train, and Thaw had to buy a box for him and ship him by freight.

At camp, Whiskey behaved like a dog after all. He followed the fliers around and climbed up on their laps to lick their faces. He made friends with real dogs, once they stopped being afraid of him, and played with them for hours at a time. His quarters were at an inn, where he was the favorite of the landlord's daughter. She tied a red ribbon around his neck and fed him bread and milk. All was well until Whiskey started acting like a cat instead of a dog. He tested his claws by scratching the coverings of sofas and ripping the curtains until they hung in ribbons. The cub was about ten times as big as an ordinary cat by now, and he did more than ten times as much damage. He wasn't welcome at the inn any more. The landlord sent word to the fliers to come get their pet before all of his furniture was ruined, so Whiskey moved to the barracks of the Escadrille.

Living with his friends was just what Whiskey wanted. Where they were was home for him. He'd been born in captivity and never known what it was to be a wild beast. Lions caught young

can be tamed and trained, as the ancient Egyptians had proved. So, though Whiskey had now grown large, he was still an affectionate, playful pet.

News spread that the Americans of the Escadrille had a live lion as a mascot. When French soldiers flocked to camp to see him, Lieutenant Lufberry decided to play a trick on the visitors. He and Whiskey hid behind a building and waited. When they saw a curious Frenchman walking by, "Luf" gave the mascot a signal. Whiskey bounded out, put his big paws on the visitor's back and bore him to the ground. The man lay there in terror,

with the lion crouched over him, showing yellow fangs in a grin. As soon as Whiskey let him up the Frenchman left camp in a hurry; though he didn't care much for the American idea of a joke, he was glad to be alive.

When Whiskey was about a year old the Escadrille found a young lioness to be his mate, and named her Soda. The pair got on beautifully. They made the camp lively as they chased each other through tents, knocking down poles and collapsing canvas on the men inside. The two playful lions helped mightily to keep up the spirit of the fliers of the Escadrille, worn out by the strain of combat in the air and saddened by the death of comrades in battle.

After the United States joined the Allies in the war, Americans in the Escadrille were transferred to their own country's Air Corps. They might not have been willing to make the change if they had known what was about to happen. Orders came that mascot lions would not be allowed in the American army. Whiskey and Soda must be sent away. There were tears in the fliers' eyes when their pets were carted off to the Paris zoo.

Whiskey and Soda were given good care in the zoo, and many people came to see them, but nobody petted and played with them as their masters used to do. Lonely and unhappy, they pined away. They died, said their friends of the Escadrille, of broken hearts.

In the town of Villeneuve d'Etang in France stands a tall monument to members of the Lafayette Escadrille who were killed in the war. And at its base are stone statues of two crouching lions—Whiskey and Soda, the mascots the Escadrille loved.

Poilu

THE 19TH DIVISION'S BRITISH LION

WHEN General Tom Bridges returned to the front from leave in Paris, during World War I, he brought a champagne basket with him. Officers of the British 19th Division, who thought they were going to have wine for dinner, got quite a surprise: out of the basket popped a small male lion.

The General laughed and explained that a friend had given him the cub and his sister, won as prizes at a party for the benefit of the Red Cross. Bridges had sent the female to a London zoo, but he had kept the male as a mascot. He couldn't have found a better one, since the lion is a symbol of the British Empire—a lion for England and a unicorn for Scotland being pictured on the British coat of arms.

The cub had been born in France, so Bridges named him Poilu—"the hairy one"—a nickname for French soldiers, many of whom then wore beards. Poilu grew fast, and developed a tremendous appetite. He raided camp kitchens so often that cooks had to lock up the meat. Once he looked through the window of the officers' mess hall and saw a favorite dish of his being served. There was a crash of glass, and Poilu landed on the

103

table, seized his meal in his jaws and leaped back into the garden to dine pleasantly in the open air.

Poilu's table manners improved when he was assigned a special mess officer of his own to keep him well supplied with meat. General Bridges insisted that his pet was "always a perfect gentleman," and certainly the lion acted as tame and good-tempered as could be. He followed his master around like a dog, without either a muzzle or a leash. But a lion was a wild animal to the French villagers, who took one look at Poilu wandering around loose and climbed the nearest tree. Children, kept home from school because Poilu was strolling through the streets, stared excitedly through the window at him and clapped their hands; if only he had been followed by a string of elephants and a few clowns, he would have been as good as a circus. Mules of the wagon trains, calm under bombardments, went

into a panic at sight of Poilu, and there were plenty of runaways and broken picket lines. Though the lion never did any harm, his soldier friends boasted that if he were allowed to go over the top in an attack he would surely chew up some Germans.

When the Division moved, Poilu rode in a special cage in a truck which also carried his large kennel and a wire-netting run in which he could exercise. But he was often freed for walks up to the front-line trenches, where he strolled around and visited the troops, who were always delighted to see him. "As brave as a lion" is an old saying, and Poilu lived up to it, for he never minded German shells bursting around him or bullets pinging by. He did jump aside nervously if he heard a truck rumbling up behind him, but that's a wise thing for anybody to do.

The fame of the 19th's mascot spread, and drew envy and admiration throughout the army, except from Corps Headquarters. They strongly disapproved of a lion at the front.

"Get rid of that beast," came the order.

General Bridges promptly answered, "Come and take him."

Nobody at the Corps showed the slightest enthusiasm for the job of arresting a large lion. Poilu would probably object and so would the whole 19th Division. No military police prepared for a lion hunt appeared, and the mascot stayed on duty.

When the 19th advanced and stormed the German trenches, they found a large gaping shell hole left by the retreating enemy. It looked like Poilu's great jaws when he opened them to roar or yawn, so the men named it "The Lion's Mouth" in his honor.

One day the British Prime Minister, Herbert Asquith, came

to visit the Division's command post. As he was being escorted through the trenches, he met Poilu face to face. Lions were to be expected in Africa, not at the front in France. But the dignified gentleman only raised his eyebrows and, saying never a word, walked on at a stately pace. It was not until the Prime Minister was leaving at the end of his tour that he asked General Bridges, with true British reserve: "I may be wrong, but did I see a lion in the path?"

Poilu might have finished out the war with the 19th if General Bridges hadn't been severely wounded and compelled to turn over his command and go to the hospital. The new commander declared there was trouble enough without a lion around. Poilu was shipped back to England, escorted by two of Bridges' aides and a bombardier.

That was an exciting trip even for wartime. Poilu seemed not to want to go home while his Division was still fighting in France. Aboard a ship crossing the English Channel, he broke out of his crate and chased passengers and crew up onto the bridge and into the rigging. At last Poilu's escorts persuaded him to occupy a first-class cabin, and, shut in there, the lion was quiet for the rest of the voyage.

In England, Poilu was given a home in the private zoo of Sir Garrand Tyrwhitt-Drake, a wild-animal expert, who made the mistake of turning his charge over to a lady lion-tamer. Poilu had always been a man's lion, and he disliked his new keeper so strongly that when she entered his cage, he bit her where she sat down.

But Poilu made friends with Sir Garrand, who praised him as the finest and most famous of the hundred lions he had owned.

Still Poilu seemed lonely, so a Great Dane was brought in to keep him company. After they had made friends through the bars of the cage, the dog was put inside. The pair got on beautifully until the Dane began to bully his companion and even dared to steal his dinner. Onlookers gasped. Great Danes are a giant breed of dog, but no match for a full-grown lion. But Poilu only looked hurt—that was no way for a friend to act—and forgave the thief. Nevertheless the rash dog was hastily removed from the cage. Next time the lion might be hungrier, and the Great Dane, after stealing a dinner, would end up by being one.

Poilu was happy when he was given a lioness mate. He became the father of several litters of cubs and lived to be nineteen years old, the pride of the zoo.

Muriel

PIG OF THE INNISKILLINGS

ONE DAY in 1919, soldiers of the Royal Inniskilling Fusiliers caught a small pig in the jungle near their barracks at Silacot, India. They named her Muriel and took good care of her. It was a funny sight to watch Muriel cradled like a baby in the arms of a big Irishman while he fed her milk from a bottle.

Soon Muriel outgrew the bottle and began to drink whole tubs of milk and eat troughsful of the finest food her soldier friends could buy for her. Nobody put her on a diet, and before long she developed into a huge animal, weighing four hundred pounds.

But food wasn't all that Muriel cared about. She loved the Inniskillings devotedly. No pigpen would do for *her* home. She lived in one of the company bungalows with her friends and always minded her manners, like a well-trained dog or cat. Music was her delight, and she never missed a concert or a dress parade. The minute the band struck up, Muriel would waddle out, take her place beside the drum major and march with the musicians, keeping up with them in spite of her short legs. As the mascot of an Irish regiment she was dressed up for St. Patrick's Day with yards of green ribbon, tied in a great bow around her fat neck.

Muriel was allowed to roam wherever she chose, except on Sunday mornings. Then she was shut up because she insisted on going to church. But even heavy doors couldn't always keep the strong pig closed in. She often broke out and trotted straight to the nearest church to find her soldier friends—and music. As the Inniskillings sat listening to the sermon they would hear grunts outside, and in would walk Muriel. Recognizing her comrades, she would utter joyful *oinks* and loud, happy squeals. It was useless to try to chase or shove her out. She would stand like the Rock of Gibraltar and refuse to budge. Finally a bandboy would be sent outside to beat a tin plate with a spoon. That was Muriel's special signal for dinner, the only call tempting enough to persuade her to leave the church.

When the Inniskillings were ordered to travel by railroad to a new post, they were told Muriel couldn't go with them. They tried their best to get her on the train by putting her down on the passenger list under the heading of Horses and Mules, but the railway officials insisted that "pigs is pigs." The adjutant of the regiment thought Muriel's friends had given up trying to take her with them until he saw Company A marching to the station beside a bullock cart.

> On it was quite the largest crate I have ever seen, its sides covered with hessian sacking [the adjutant wrote]. Accompanying the cart was a crowd of troops who were making the most awful noise, shouting and singing. Above it I could hear infuriated grunts coming from inside the crate. The louder the grunts became, the louder was the row put up by the troops. I gathered that Muriel was being smuggled onto the train, and the male chorus was assembled to drown the sounds of her protest.

Twenty men heaved the crate aboard, and Muriel, well-guarded, made the seven-day journey as comfortably as if she had been a prize race horse.

At Belgaum, the new post, Muriel became more than ever the pride of the Inniskillings. She evidently thought she had been entered in the Senior Officers' School, for she enthusiastically attended all classes and exercises. Cross-country runs were her favorite sport. In spite of her enormous size, she was so fast and agile that she got over all obstacles, and always finished fifth or sixth in a field of two hundred men runners. She joined in bayonet charges and hurtled forward with the assault wave, squealing like mad. An enemy, said the Inniskillings, would have stood up better to a tank than to those four hundred pounds of charging pig.

Muriel, serving in peacetime, never had a chance to show what she could have done in a war. But when she strolled through a city, streetcars and automobiles gave her the right of way or stopped with grinding brakes to escape being wrecked on Muriel.

Plans were made to sneak Muriel aboard ship when the Inniskillings were ordered to sail to Iraq in 1924. Unfortunately the crate trick could not be worked again. The pig had to be given to an artillery regiment. From the dock she watched her friends' ship sail, and squealed a forlorn farewell.

Poor Muriel! The artillerymen didn't believe what the Inniskillings had told them about her—that she was a music-lover, a bandleader, a churchgoer, a cross-country runner and worth her weight in assault troops. They saw her only as hams, bacon, spareribs and pork chops, and they ate her for Christmas dinner.

111

Young Abe

EAGLE OF THE 101ST AIRBORNE DIVISION

SOLDIER CLERKS filled in a service record for a new member that had just joined the 101st Airborne Division, grinning as they wrote down these words:

> Name: Young Abe.
> Serial Number: 5555555.
> Drafted at Portage, Wisconsin, 1942.
> Medical Examination: Passed. No fleas.
> Age: Four years.
> Height: Two feet, ten inches.
> Weight: Twenty-five pounds.
> Eyes: Black. Hair: White.
> Military Specialty: Making noise.

That read like an odd description of a recruit, but it fitted Young Abe. He was an eagle.

Young Abe had been appointed the Division's mascot, and everyone agreed he was a splendid choice. Eagles are warlike birds, and images of them have been perched on the top of standards armies have carried into battle from the days of the Roman legions on. Our forefathers voted for the eagle as the

American national bird, even though Benjamin Franklin thought the turkey would have been better. An eagle like Young Abe was pictured on the Great Seal of the United States, and on bills and coins. Every payday the men of the 101st would be pleasantly reminded of their mascot. Best of all, a high-flying, fighting bird that swooped down out of clouds onto enemies seemed ideal as a mascot for airborne troops who would go into action the same way.

Why was he called Young Abe? soldiers asked. Because, the Division newspaper explained, he was the namesake of Old Abe, the famous eagle of the 8th Wisconsin Regiment in the Civil War, a mascot which had been named after Abraham Lincoln. It might be that the two eagles had more in common than a name, for both had been caught in the Wisconsin woods near the same place. They might even belong to the same family. Markings on Young Abe's brown feathers were much like those shown in photographs of Old Abe. Perhaps this young bird was a great-grandson of Old Abe's parents. In any event, the Airborne Division's mascot had an inspiring example before him and a fine record to try to equal. Old Abe's bearers had carried him through thirty-six battles.

It was a great day when Young Abe was officially accepted as the mascot of the 101st in a ceremony at Fort Bragg, North Carolina. Paratroopers, and infantry and artillery regiments which would be flown to battlefields by means of planes and gliders, marched out on the big parade ground. Commands rang out, the band struck up and flags fluttered in the wind.

Now came Young Abe's moment. White crest held high, brown plumage sleek, he gripped his staff perch with strong

113

talons and was carried forward by his bearer, a master sergeant. He took his proud post between the Stars and Stripes and the banner of the 101st. Wisconsin men were the color-guards. As movie cameras clicked and radio broadcasters spoke into their microphones, Young Abe looked from side to side and majestically extended his mighty wings in their eight-foot spread just as Old Abe used to do. Fort Bragg echoed to the cheers of the watching crowds.

General William C. Lee, the Division Commander, saluting the colors and the eagle, made a speech:

> Because our Division is airborne and destined to fly into battle through the airlanes of the sky, the symbol of the great American eagle seems to us especially appropriate. We thank the State of Wisconsin for this splendid bird. Young Abe will be a constant reminder to us all of the symbol for which he stands. We shall try to be worthy of that symbol.

While the Division went on with its training, Young Abe began his. He was allowed to fly the length of the tether that tied him to his perch, but he wasn't freed to soar into the skies. His trainers weren't yet sure he would return, as Old Abe always had. Meanwhile he was fed plenty of fresh meat so he would want to come home and not fly away to the woods and turn into a wild eagle again.

One evening a live hen was put into his cage for his dinner. But Young Abe's fondness for her company was greater than his appetite. Next morning the two were found nestling side by side, and the hen had gratefully laid an egg for her host.

Young Abe's story cannot tell that he went overseas with the

114

101st and dropped with its paratroopers from the skies to go into action against the enemy. Nor that he perched on General McAuliffe's shoulder when that officer refused the German demand for surrender at Bastogne in the Battle of the Bulge. Those were only might-have-beens. What really happened was

that the eagle died from some unknown illness before the Division went off to war.

But every soldier of the gallant 101st carried Young Abe's picture with him. On the shoulder patch of their uniform was embroidered the snowy crest, flashing eye and fierce curved beak of their mascot, the American eagle. They still proudly wear that badge today.

115

G.I. Joe

FROM THE DAY the pigeon pecked his way out of his egg, it was almost certain that he would join the army. He was born into it, bred from Signal Corps homing pigeons. As soon as he grew old enough he would be enlisted and begin his flight training.

His feathers were white, with dark marks like a checkerboard's. Pigeoneers in charge of the loft where he lived wrote down on their records that this "squeaker," as they called him, was a pied white cock pigeon. Around his legs they fastened two metal bands marked with his birth date and his army serial number. But a string of numbers didn't seem enough for such a bright and willing bird, so they gave him a name too—G.I. Joe.

G.I. Joe had that marvelous instinct which has belonged to homing pigeons for centuries—a wonderful urge and sense of direction that guides them home over long distances. It brought the dove that Noah sent out to find dry land back to the Ark. The Greeks, Romans, Saracens and many other nations used homing pigeons to carry messages in peace or war. Once a homer flew from Arras, France, to Saigon, Indo-China—7200 miles—in twenty-four days. Now, in 1942, many thousands of these remarkable birds were being trained for war service. Sometimes not even radio or airplanes could take their place, for pigeons could fly in bad weather that grounded planes and put radios out of action.

To train G.I. Joe, pigeoneers loaded his cage on a truck and drove away from the loft, at first a short distance and later many miles. The minute he was freed he rose in the air and flew straight back home like an arrow. Down he fluttered, and "trapped" or pushed through the trap door of his own cubbyhole in the loft, where he ate the grain he learned to know would be waiting for him. When he was older he was given a mate, and his longing to return to her and their nest made him fly home even faster.

G.I. Joe might have been assigned to the Air Forces. There he would have learned how to drop from a plane in a paper bag until he fell past the dangerous blast from the propeller—then to burst out of the bag and take wing. Or he might have become a pigeon paratrooper and been taught to float down to the ground, borne by his own small parachute to troops who needed a messenger.

As it turned out, G.I. Joe was chosen to serve with the Infantry because he wasn't nervous under fire and could be counted on to be fast and sure in delivering a message. He always finished his flights, no matter how tired he was. His trainers said he was like the Fort Bliss pigeon which, when he was caught by someone who clipped his wings, escaped and walked back to his loft.

G.I. Joe was made a member of the 209th Signal Pigeon

Company and sent overseas to Italy. He was with the Fifth Army when it landed at Salerno and broke through German beach defenses, and the Americans and British began to fight their way inland.

He and other pigeons were traveling along with the troops in a truck called a mobile loft when the British asked if they could borrow one of the birds. It was G.I. Joe whose cage was lifted out and given to the 169th Brigade of the British 56th Infantry Division. They carried him forward when they attacked the village of Colve Vecchio, strongly held by the Germans.

When the brigade failed to drive the Germans out, it sent a call by radio for planes to bomb the enemy. But before that help could come, the brigade made another attack, and this time succeeded in taking the village. Now the bombers would have to be stopped. Unless word reached the airfield quickly, tons of high explosive, intended for the Nazis, would fall on the British who had captured Colve Vecchio. A signaler frantically worked his radio, but in vain. It had blacked out and was useless.

There was just one hope left of sending a message that might arrive in time—G.I. Joe. Many lives depended on him. Hands took him gently from his cage and thrust a hastily scribbled message into a holder strapped to his right leg. Then he was lifted up and given flight.

Shells burst and bullets whistled around the homer as he spiraled upward and circled until his instinct told him where to go. Back to the mobile loft he darted. He flew the twenty miles to it in twenty minutes. The instant he trapped, a pigeoneer whisked the message from its holder and ran to headquarters.

Bombers were about to take off when a colonel rushed up to

the leading plane, shouting, "Hold it! A British brigade has just entered Colve Vecchio." A few minutes more and it would have been too late to halt a bombing which would have killed many soldiers of the 169th.

The grateful British never forgot G.I. Joe. After the war they asked that he be allowed to come to England for a visit. An American plane flew him to London, where he was met by a representative of the U.S. Embassy, the secretary of the Allied Forces Mascot Club and a British officer who was chief of the Air Ministry Pigeon Section. They gave him comfortable quarters in the loft of the International Congress of Pigeon Fanciers.

After a few days of rest, G.I. Joe was taken to the Green of the Tower of London. There the visitor was welcomed by a British field marshal, an American major general, and many others, while scarlet-clad Yeomen of the Guard stood at attention to do him honor. G.I. Joe looked out from his traveling cage with round bright eyes and seemed to be listening modestly as an officer read the report of his splendid flight from Colve Vecchio to halt the bombers. British General Keightly made a speech that ended: "Well done, G.I. Joe!" Then he lifted the pigeon out and slipped over his head the green, brown and blue ribbon of the Dickin Medal, which is called "The Animals' Victoria Cross." Though G.I. Joe could not read the words on the medal, FOR GALLANTRY—THEY ALSO SERVED, everyone thought he looked proud to have it.

The veteran homing pigeon was flown back to the United States. When he was retired, he was given quarters at the Pigeon Breeding and Training Center at Fort Monmouth, New Jersey. Many admiring callers came to see him. Every year G.I. Joe and his mate raised two broods of fine young homing pigeons, which, like their father, grew up to carry messages for the army.

Some pigeons live long lives—like Kaiser, a German army messenger which was captured by our soldiers in the Battle of the Argonne during the First World War and brought back to the United States. Every year children at Fort Monmouth gave a party for Kaiser on his birthday in February. He died when he was thirty-two years old. Many of the pigeons he fathered, twenty-five generations of them, served in the Second World War.

As this story is written, G.I. Joe, about thirteen years old, is in excellent health and living in honored and happy retirement in his loft at Fort Monmouth.

Minnie

PONY OF THE LANCASHIRE FUSILIERS

A PACK - PONY MARE plodded through the jungles of
Burma, in the baggage train of the 77th British Infantry Brigade. It was 1944, during the Second World War. The packers
glanced anxiously at the pony, for it was plain that she was
going to have a foal before long. Nobody knew how it had happened. Every animal on this dangerous expedition behind the
Japanese lines had been specially picked to stand hardships and
privations. If it had been known that the pony was going to
become a mother, she would never have been taken along.

But it was too late to do anything about it now. The packers
wouldn't abandon the pony to be eaten by tigers or other wild
beasts, so they lightened her load, distributing parts of it among
other ponies and mules. She marched on with the 77th as it
slipped past the Japanese and built a fortified camp to block an
important road and railroad line.

Quickly the blockade was discovered, and the Japanese attacked furiously. While shells from their artillery burst over
the British trenches and gun positions, the pack-pony's foal began to be born. Sergeant Lee of the 1st Battalion, Lancashire

Fusiliers, left the defense line to help the mare, and soon a fine little filly, black with white markings, arrived. Lee named her after a mortar, called "Minnie," which had been in action nearby when she came into the world.

News of the birth of a pony in the midst of the battle spread through the "Block." As soon as the fighting was over, soldiers off duty flocked around to see Minnie. Staggering up on wobbly legs to drink her mother's milk, she was an appealing sight. Troopers crowded forward to pat the white blaze on her forehead until Sergeant Lee made them leave and let her rest.

Minnie and her mother were with the other animals on the transport picket lines when the Japanese attacked again. Shells of a heavy bombardment crashed around them. Several mules were killed and others broke loose. One of them, frantic with terror, kicked Minnie in the head, severely injuring her right eye.

Again Sergeant Lee came to the rescue. He was a British Gypsy and, like many of his people, he loved horses and knew how to doctor them. Night and day he took tender care of the little filly, stunned and shocked by the terrible blow from the mule's hoof.

Brigadier Calvert, the Commanding Officer, not only came himself to see how the pony was, but ordered that regular bulletins reporting Minnie's condition be sent to all companies of the brigade. At last Minnie's anxious friends heard the good news that she was recovering, and that the sergeant had succeeded in saving the sight of her eye.

When Minnie grew stronger she strolled around camp to pay calls on her soldier friends, as if to thank them for wishing her well. They gave her a royal welcome and brewed tea for her, which she drank by the pint-potful. She amused and entertained everyone by doing clever tricks Sergeant Lee had taught her.

Meanwhile a strong Japanese army had closed in and threatened to overwhelm the "Block." Brigadier Calvert ordered a retreat. His men could fight their way out, and there was transportation for the wounded. But what would become of Minnie? She was still too small and weak to make the exhausting march through the jungle with her mother and the rest of the pack train. The whole brigade was distressed over what might happen to her.

Brigadier Calvert understood how much Minnie meant to his troops—how much she had cheered up everyone and endeared herself during those weeks of hard fighting. Minnie must be taken out by air, he decided. He radioed for a light plane, then gave orders that the Japanese be driven away from the airstrip. A gallant attack pushed the enemy farther back into the jungle, and the strip was clear. When the plane came in and landed, willing hands lifted Minnie aboard. Soldiers watched tensely and sighed with relief as the plane took off and darted away, unhit by Japanese rifle and machine-gun fire. It carried Minnie safely to India.

Months later Sergeant Lee and the rest of the Lancashire Fusiliers, having fought their way out of Burma with the brigade, joined Minnie in India for a happy reunion. The Fusiliers had been her special comrades, since Lee had helped at her birth and cured her eye, and now she became their official mascot. More than that, she seemed to believe that she commanded the battalion. She marched at its head in parades, wearing a handsome saddle cloth, a browband decorated with the regimental crest, and gay-colored leggings. She faithfully attended drills, but if they seemed to her too long she would trot up behind Sergeant Lee and nudge him in the back. When the adjutant saw the impatient pony, he would grin and dismiss the battalion, although it was half an hour too early.

Minnie often visited barracks for a treat of buns and tea. She had to be watched or she would walk into mess halls and eat everything on the table, including the cloth. At parties for the benefit of charity, Minnie was the star money-raiser. She circulated among the guests with a collection box strapped to her back; it was soon stuffed full of bills and coins. Children whose parents made contributions were given rides on the famous mascot pony.

A day came when money was needed for Minnie herself. Trucks replaced mules as the Fusiliers' transport, and Minnie

no longer had stablemates to share their feed with her. There wasn't enough in the battalion fund to pay for the pony's keep or for her passage back to England with the Fusiliers, who had been ordered home.

Lieutenant Colonel Jackson promptly started a Minnie Fund. All the people Minnie had helped to raise money paid to come to a big party for her benefit. Every payday the pony marched to each company, escorted by drummers. Officers and men gladly contributed something for their beloved mascot.

So, in 1947, the pony born in the Burma jungle happily sailed with her comrades to a new home in England.

G.I. Jenny

FIFTH U.S. ARMY DONKEY

THE TINY DONKEY, born in North Africa, was lucky. When she was only two weeks old she was bought from her Arab owner for two thousand francs by Headquarters soldiers of the Fifth U.S. Army. They made her their mascot and named her G.I. Jenny. By becoming an American pet in the Second World War, Jenny escaped the fate of most other donkeys in her native land. In Africa, as soon as she grew strong enough, her life work would have been carrying her bearded Arab master, his legs and flowing robes almost touching the ground as he sat astride the little donkey. On her back behind her rider would have been slung baskets of food and household goods. Almost hidden by that heavy burden, she would have plodded countless miles over white roads or across the desert while the Arab's veiled womenfolk and children trudged along behind.

Instead, Jenny lived a life of ease and plenty. She never had to carry anybody or anything. On marches, kind-hearted Fifth Army men picked her up in their arms and carried her when she was tired. Later on she rode in style in a jeep, waggling her long ears and enjoying herself immensely. At first she was fed

127

on condensed milk, but she soon began to eat grain and hay. She loved candy bars for dessert, and nuzzled for them in the pockets of every soldier she met. If she was still hungry, and she usually was, she ate anything she found—grass, orange peel and all the paper in the scrapbaskets of the Red Cross clubs. Of course that didn't agree with her, and she had to answer sick call often until the veterinary ordered her put on a strict diet.

There were other animals in camp: dogs, a fawn, a monkey, a hedgehog and a rabbit. But mouse-colored, thick-coated little G.I. Jenny was everybody's favorite. Soldiers were her best friends, and she would stand up for them as strongly as they would for her. She quickly learned to tell the difference between soldiers and officers. Officers, she noticed, were people who ordered her special pals around and bothered them. Jenny didn't like that and she showed it.

Once, at a Saturday inspection, she watched a company commander stride along the lines, finding fault and bawling out men in the ranks. Jenny stamped her small feet and laid back her ears. Then she lowered her head, charged and butted the officer in the rear with all her might. He staggered forward and fell flat. Only Arab boys on the side lines dared laugh as Jenny's victim picked himself up from the dust. The company stood stiffly at attention, every man's face red with his effort to keep from howling with glee and giving three cheers for Jenny. But after they were dismissed, the grateful G.I.'s led the donkey triumphantly back to barracks and feasted her on all the candy bars she could eat.

Jenny was no more respectful toward generals. If a big staff car, carrying officers with stars on their helmets, drove toward

her, she would plant herself in its path and refuse to budge. It did no good to coax her and even less to shout at her. Jenny took orders from no one ranking higher than a private, or perhaps a sergeant. Finally she would kick up her heels, flip her ears impudently, step aside and let the generals, grinning, drive on.

But Jenny as the Fifth Army mascot would sometimes condescend to appear on the same platform with the Commanding General when he made a speech to the troops. If he talked too long, though, she acted distinctly bored. Also, she liked to walk into the ring between rounds of boxing bouts and take a bow. Her knowing look seemed to say, "This is a pretty good fight, but you ought to have seen me the day I socked that captain at inspection!"

Jenny landed at Salerno, Italy, with troops of the Fifth Army and stayed with them through the hard fighting there and at Anzio and on the Po River. She behaved so bravely and faithfully that she was promoted to be a corporal and wore her two stripes along with the Fifth Army badge on her blanket.

After the war was over and troops of the Fifth Army began to leave for the United States, Jenny's friends decided they couldn't bear to leave her behind in Italy. Though they were told she wouldn't be allowed on their ship, they planned to sneak her aboard and hide her. Laban P. Jackson, one of Jenny's oldest comrades, promised to give her a good home on his Hereford cattle farm in Kentucky.

But Jenny's luck had run out. Just two days before sailing, she trotted in front of a truck which struck her and broke one of her forelegs. Not only the veterinaries but all the doctors and even the dentists at Headquarters did their best to save her. They put her leg in a cast but it wouldn't heal, and she had to be painlessly destroyed.

It was a shame Corporal Jenny did not live to stroll around among the big brown-and-white Herefords in Kentucky and treat them as impudently as she had generals. But she does live as a happy memory in the hearts of veterans of the Fifth Army.

Scrappy and Tuffy

WILDCATS OF THE 81ST U.S. DIVISION

THE WILDCAT'S fierce yellow eyes, gleaming in the moonlight, glared from a tree branch in a Carolina mountain forest. He hooked sharp claws into the bark of the trunk and clambered down to the ground, for his hunger was driving him to catch a fat quail or two for his supper. But his journey that night was to have a different ending.

He looked like a brownish-red, overgrown house cat except for his tufted ears and short, stubby tail. As he prowled through the woods, larger animals left him strictly alone. So would men unless they faced him with a ready rifle or shotgun, for all wildcats are savage fighters.

At last the hungry wildcat sniffed the scent of meat and pounced eagerly. Too late he discovered that meat, tied inside a loop of rope, was bait in a trap. The other end of the rope was fastened to a bent-down sapling, and when the wildcat grabbed for his meal, the young tree was released and sprang upward. It tightened the noose around the beast's neck like a lasso and jerked him into the air. There he hung helpless, but he was still full of fight the next morning when the trappers came. With

132

guns pointed in case the snarling, spitting captive might wriggle free, they lowered him into a strong wooden box, which was loaded into a wagon and carried to Camp Jackson, South Carolina.

There the 81st Division was in training for the First World War. When the box was delivered at headquarters, the wagon driver announced, "Here's a mascot for you. It's a wildcat. Handle with care."

"Don't handle at all" was better advice still, and soldiers followed it when they found out that the wildcat welcomed no advances. He bit and clawed at anyone who came near him, and was so plainly ready for a scrap that he quickly earned the name Scrappy. Food had to be pushed into his cage with a pole, and the longer the pole, the safer.

But men of the 81st liked Scrappy's fighting spirit, and de-

cided to take him along when they were ordered overseas. The wildcat in his cage was hoisted aboard one of their transports. Unfortunately, though, Scrappy was one of those wild animals that cannot stand captivity. During the Atlantic crossing he became sick and died, and was buried at sea.

Yet Scrappy's likeness was still with the Division. It had been embroidered on patches which men of the 81st wore on the left sleeves of their coats and overcoats.

Shoulder patches had never before been used in the United States Army and were not according to regulations. Inspecting officers took one look at them when the Division landed in France, and bristled like the wildcats on the patches. "Rip those things off!" they ordered.

But General Pershing, the Commander-in-Chief of the American Expeditionary Forces, disagreed with his inspectors and decided that the patches were an excellent idea. They set the men of an organization apart from others and made them proud to belong to it. When soldiers made a good record in combat, they would be prouder still of their emblem and strive harder to live up to it. So General Pershing not only allowed the Wildcat Division to keep its patches but issued an order that every division in the army must adopt one of its own. That was the beginning of the bright-colored patches of many different designs worn by all the Armed Services today.

The 81st carried the sign of the wildcat into battle in France. When peace came, its men put away their uniforms with the shoulder patches on them.

Twenty-four years later the 81st Division was reorganized to fight in the Second World War, and again embroidered wildcats appeared on olive-drab sleeves. This time they pictured a new mascot, presented by the Governor of Georgia—a wildcat cub which veterans declared was the spitting image of Scrappy but even tougher. They named the cub Tuffy and put him in a roofed cage near the parade ground. Up and down Tuffy stalked like a sentry, challenging all comers with snap and vim. He did have a soft side, though, for he liked women visitors, and when they stopped to admire him, his snarling changed into a resounding purr.

Wooden statues of Tuffy decorated the roofs of barracks, and the camp was nicknamed "Lair of Wildcats." Two more bobcats (as wildcats are often called) were added to the Division's mascot menagerie, but Tuffy, the largest and fiercest, remained the favorite and was the only one of the three that went along when the troops were ordered to Arizona for desert training.

There, under a scorching summer sun that pushed the heat up to 126 degrees in the shade, man and beast wilted. Tuffy's distant cousin, the African lion, could have weathered it, but the mountain cat had to be sprinkled with cold water to pull him through the hottest part of the day. He grew so irritable that his orderly no longer dared reach a hand through the bars of his cage to stroke his head.

Then the Division moved west with sailing orders for the campaign against Japan. At the port of embarkation Major General Paul J. Mueller asked whether the men he commanded would be allowed to take their mascot with them.

Take a live wildcat? Never, was the answer. Tuffy, the Division learned sadly, would have to be left behind.

Then veterans of the 81st remembered how General Pershing

135

had let them keep their shoulder patch in 1918. A request for permission to take Tuffy overseas was sent to the head of the War Department, and Secretary Stimson promptly granted it. Tuffy was the living symbol of the 81st's fighting spirit, he answered, and the Wildcat Division certainly must have its wildcat with it.

So Tuffy embarked with his outfit and sailed across the Pacific to Hawaii. But more trouble was waiting for him there. He was held in animal quarantine, and this time no appeal could free him until his time was up. The law was so strict that even President Roosevelt, when he arrived a little later with his dog Fala, had to leave his pet aboard ship in Honolulu harbor.

Though the troops of the 81st had to go to war without Tuffy, his fighting spirit went with them. From landing craft they stormed ashore on Angaur Island, near Peliliu, drove the Japanese from their beach defenses and coral caves and mopped them up in the jungle. It was a good Division—brave men, well led—and it fought with a fury that was true to its motto: "A Wildcat never quits. He wins or he dies."

When Tuffy's quarantine ended, he was shipped on to rejoin his Division in New Caledonia, where the men had been sent to rest. In his jeep-mounted cage he toured the area and paid a visit to every camp. Whenever troops were paraded, he rode behind the colors while the band played a march composed in his honor. Generals and admirals inspected Tuffy's muscles and glossy coat from a safe distance and pronounced him as fit as any soldier in the Division. But the wildcat showed no respect for rank and snarled viciously at the officers to the delight of watching G.I.'s.

136

The mascot and his Division weren't parted again during the war. Tuffy was present for duty in the Philippines and during the occupation of Japan. After some months, the length of his service entitled him to go home. General Mueller gave him travel orders and instructed an aide, Lieutenant Frank Pidgeon, Jr.:

> It is my wish and that of all Wildcats of the 81st Infantry Division, who have a lot of sentiment for that beautiful but mean cat, that en route you provide him with all the comforts to which he has been accustomed. With us he saw this war to a victorious conclusion. He well deserves retirement after three and one-half years of arduous service.

Tuffy and his escort enjoyed a pleasant voyage to San Francisco. Railway expressmen, careful to keep away from his claws, put him aboard an eastbound train. Roomy quarters, marked with his name and army record, were given him in the zoo at Memphis, Tennesee, and there the veteran settled down in his old soldier's home. Many visitors came to see him, and to the end of his days Tuffy remained one of the most popular and admired animals in the zoo.

Simon

BRITISH NAVY CAT

SINCE KITTENHOOD Simon had been the ship's cat of
the British gunboat *Amethyst*. If words had been put to his
purring, surely they would have sounded like a song from
Pinafore.

> I sail the ocean blue,
> And my saucy ship's a beauty.
> A sober cat and true
> And attentive to my duty.

On the leather collar around his neck Simon wore an identity
disk, a tag with his name on it. He was rated on the ship's pa-
pers as a Royal Animal Auxiliary, and he acted as if he understood that Auxiliary meant being helpful. Always he kept
himself looking trim and shipshape by washing his white muzzle, chest, forepaws and black coat with his long pink tongue.
He would climb up on the chart table to help the skipper lay a
course—or at least not hinder him too much. Often he would
inspect gun deck and forecastle, visiting sailor friends. When his
watch was over, he would curl up and go to sleep in a petty

officer's cap. But Simon never failed to be present for guard duty when the *Amethyst* made port and rats crept up the cables to come aboard. Then Simon would pounce fiercely, repelling boarders, or hunt down any rat that had slipped past him.

It was in 1949, when the *Amethyst* sailed from Hong Kong, China, up the yellow Yangtze River, that the great days of Simon's career came. The Chinese Communists, who were fighting the Chinese Nationalists, had given permission to the gunboat to steam upriver to Nanking with supplies for the British Embassy. But the Communists broke their promise. Their artillery batteries on shore opened a terrific fire on the *Amethyst* that killed seventeen of her crew and wounded ten, including the captain, who was so badly hurt that he died. Simon, too, was hit by shell fragments in the face and back. He dragged himself to a corner of the hold to nurse his wounds.

The British warship's guns blazed back at the shore batteries, and she tried to steam out of range of the Chinese fire, but her steering gear had been knocked out, and she ran aground on Rose Island. The brave Britons still manned their guns and worked hard on repairs. Lieutenant Commander Kerans flew in by seaplane to take the dead captain's place.

Simon, in spite of his wound, came back on duty, for big, hungry rats had swarmed aboard from the island. Simon tore into them with tooth and claw. The crew kept his score on the bulletin board, and it was always at least one kill a day. Between hunts he visited his friends at the guns to be petted and praised. For three dreadful months under fire, Simon battled as gallantly as his shipmates. All hands realized what splendid

139

service the cat was doing. If it had not been for his mighty efforts, the rats would have eaten up a good deal of the ship's food, which was running dangerously low.

At last the stranded gunboat completed repairs, steamed clear and fought her way down the river to the safety of Hong Kong. There a grand welcome was waiting, and not for a moment was Simon forgotten. Commander Kerans—who was given a medal and promoted—had sent a glowing report, commending the cat "for his determined attitude which did much to improve crew morale and for behaviour of the highest order during the whole of the Yangtze incident." King George wirelessed his congratulations to all. While the crew drank their Sovereign's health, Simon joined in and lapped up a saucer of milk.

That was just the first of the valiant cat's rewards. Newspapers had told his story, and from all over the world came cables and letters for him, along with presents of canned fish and money to buy him cream and ribbons.

When the *Amethyst* arrived back home to England, her crew paraded through cheering crowds, but Simon could not be with them. The law required him to stay in quarantine long enough to make sure he had no disease which might spread to other cats. Meanwhile reporters came to see him and write his story, with photographers to take his picture. Then it was announced with a fanfare that Simon was going to receive the Dickin Medal—the Animals' Victoria Cross. That decoration had previously been conferred on fifty-three horses and dogs and one American pigeon, G.I. Joe. Never before had it been won by a cat.

Sad to say, Simon, weakened by his wound, caught cold and

140

SCORE

died before the medal was given to him, but it was awarded in his memory. He was buried in a pet cemetery in Plymouth, his ship's home port, beneath a stone on which his head is sculptured over the line: "In Honoured Memory of Simon, D.M." (Dickin Medal). Friends and admirers gave money to establish a Simon Memorial Fund for the benefit of families of sailors killed in the Yangtze battle and for the men who had been disabled. The money is used also to help the work of the People's Dispensary for Sick Animals of the Poor.

Simon's Dickin Medal hangs today in the wardroom of the *Amethyst.* The colors of its ribbon are green for the grass where war dogs scout; brown for the mud and sand through which horses and mules pull guns and wagons, and blue for the air where carrier pigeons fly and for the sea Simon sailed. On one bronze face of the medal is Simon's name and that of his ship. On the other are the words: "For Gallantry. We Also Serve." How truly Simon deserved that!

William

BUFFALO OF THE 17TH INFANTRY

"HOW ARE those buffaloes doing up there, Buffalo Bill?"

The Commanding General of the 7th U.S. Division was talking on the field telephone to a colonel of front-line troops in Korea, one February day in 1951. Back over the line came an answer from Colonel Bill Quinn: "Sir, the buffaloes are stampeding the North Koreans."

Of course there were no real buffaloes in Korea. "Buffaloes" is a nickname for the men of the 17th Infantry, a regiment with a gallant record stretching back to the War of 1812. It has fought in every U.S. war since, including combat with the Indians. Then great herds of the big shaggy animals after which the soldiers of the 17th are named thundered over the western plains.

The regiment, glad to hear that the General remembered its nickname, painted pictures of buffaloes on its jeeps, trucks, tanks and helmets. But something was still lacking, Colonel Quinn thought—a live buffalo would be a perfect mascot for the 17th. Could one be brought over from the States?

Buffaloes were scarce now. People said it was hard to find one except on a nickel. Once countless herds of buffaloes, millions of them, had roamed the Great Plains of North America. The meat of bisons (their correct name) had furnished the Indian tribes with food, while hides supplied the red man's clothing and the walls of his wigwams. Yet their numbers had scarcely diminished until white hunters came and shot them down in a wholesale slaughter for buffalo robes for carriages and sleighs, and meat for railroad-builders. So many of the great humped beasts were killed that they became almost extinct. Fortunately the survivors—only about a thousand—were protected, and now small herds in national parks and on private ranches were increasing.

Colonel Quinn remembered reading of a ranch in Kansas that raised buffaloes. Promptly he wrote a letter to the owner, Gene Clark, offering to purchase one animal from his herd.

Back came the answer from Mr. Clark that he would be delighted to make a present of a buffalo to a famous regiment fighting in Korea. He said that he had already picked out and rounded up a husky bull calf named William, two months old and weighing one hundred pounds. Though William was still drinking his mother's milk, when the time came for him to join his regiment he could be fed by bottle from a formula. He would remain a bottle baby until he was seven or eight months old; after that he would graze. While William waited for travel orders he would be trained to be led by a halter so he could march with his regiment.

Then began a long, hard struggle to ship William to Korea.

144

Colonel Quinn tried the Air Force and the regular airlines, but there was no room on their planes for a buffalo calf. Senators and congressmen from Kansas vainly made pleas to the Defense and State Departments in William's behalf. They were told that cattle, which might carry hoof-and-mouth disease, could not be sent to the Far East.

But nobody was willing to give up. William's friends kept trying to wangle an overseas permit for him. Meanwhile Mr. Clark sent a series of airmail bulletins to Colonel Quinn and the 17th Infantry on the health and daily doings of their mascot.

We have a pen for him (ran Bulletin Number 1) so that the hundreds of tourists can see him and feed him. And we are having a sign made which will show his name and the fact that his owners are the men in the Buffalo Regiment. He will make the trip okay, since he is too cockeyed ornery to do anything else.

Again:

> William now weighs over four hundred pounds, making him
> the largest calf in the herd. He has found that by jumping at
> the fence he can scare heck out of people. And that is precisely
> the way he wants it.

Another report:

> Last week he got out and went down to the big pasture
> where the herd was grazing. There was a tall fence between
> him and the herd. He shadow-boxed against the fence looking
> for an opponent all day, arriving home late in the evening,
> weary and hungry.

One more:

> We have a bunch of baby chicks which have made their
> home in William's pen. He likes to lie down and let them walk
> all over him searching for any flies or bugs he might have
> acquired.

Over in Korea, soldiers of the 17th kept asking for their mascot. They volunteered to take up a collection and pay William's fare, but their offer was turned down by Headquarters. As long as permission to ship William was refused, money wouldn't help.

Meanwhile Colonel Quinn had been promoted to brigadier general and returned to the United States, where he continued his efforts to ship the mascot to his old regiment. He went to Florida to meet William, brought from Kansas in a van to be shown at the Tampa Fair. There at least William was welcomed and appreciated. He won first prize as Grand Champion Buffalo Bull, the first time in cattle-show history that a bison had ever received such an award. As was only fitting and proper, his blue ribbon was sent to the 17th in Korea.

At one time it looked as if William might follow his ribbon. He was about to be loaded into a crate for the trip when word came at the last moment that a military permit had been denied again. Arguing with the army about such matters as mascots is tough business when it's fighting a war.

So William, grown into a hefty four-hundred-pounder, had to be labeled "The Buffalo That Didn't Go." He roams the range in Kansas, waiting to join the 17th Infantry when it comes home.

Not only William will be waiting. He has become the father of a fine calf. William II has grown up and he too has a son, William III. If this keeps up, every company of the 17th Infantry will have a buffalo mascot, and a regimental review will look like a parade and a Wild West roundup combined.

Mascots in Korea

THE FULL STORIES of mascots that have served with our Armed Forces in Korea have not yet been told. Those tales will have to wait, because most of the pets will stay abroad until the last of the men of their divisions, regiments, and other units return to the United States. But here are listed some of the animals and birds which have been such good company for our soldiers, sailors, and airmen at the front and in rear areas.

The 45th Division has twin spider monkeys, and the Ordnance Company of the X Corps owns one that chews gum and wrestles with the other mascot of the company, a dog. A third monkey, Jocko, rode for a while in tanks of the 25th Division, but he monkeyed so much with the machinery that he was transferred to Headquarters.

When the French battalion left Korea for Indo-China, it turned over its goat, called Biquet, to the Headquarters Company of the 2nd American Division. For a time cooks planned to make a stew of him, but he was so lively and amusing that they couldn't bring themselves to put him on the bill of fare. Now Biquet hangs around the officers' club and begs for a glass of French wine, which he used to share with his former owners.

A duck, a pig and a rabbit are among the pets of the 27th Infantry. A donkey, named Francis after the mule in the movies, helps deliver the 14th Infantry's mail.

There are many dogs. Fighter Bomber, son of a champion German Shepherd in Japan, is the mascot of the plane carrier *Philippine Sea*. He has a tailor-made uniform he wears on special occasions. His service record, always kept up to date, says he is entitled to the Korean War ribbon with a battle star and the United Nations medal. Six battle stars are claimed for Tex of H Battery, 3rd Battalion, 11th Marines; he is the father of six puppies. The dog Combat of the Artillery, 25th Division, is famous for living up to the reputation of mascots by bringing his outfit good luck. After he joined the guns, not a single shell fired by the enemy landed in his artillery's positions.

Two of the dogs are paratroopers, or rather parapooches. Teddy has jumped with the men of the Quartermaster Airborne Air Supply and Packaging Company. Another dog, belonging to the 314th Troop Carrier Group, made a forced jump with Technical Sergeant Robert E. Ferris of Shelby, Michigan, when their C–119 caught fire. The plane exploded, but Ferris and his pet were well clear of it and landed safely. There's also a fox named Felix which jumps with the 187th Airborne Regiment.

Deer are mascots of the 2nd Infantry Division and of an Air Police detachment in Japan. The 15th Infantry, 3rd Division, has a pony, Papa-san, captured from the Chinese Reds.

Rockey, a Korean bear cub, was given by the United Nations Honor Guard to General Maxwell D. Taylor. Since Rockey would weigh 250 pounds when he grew up, the General wisely turned him back to the Guard to keep for him.

149

Among the birds are three owls, pets of the 4th Signal Battalion, the 32nd Infantry, and the Armed Forces Radio Network. Maybe the third one has been trained to hoot on broadcasts. A Japanese fishhawk landed on the hospital ship *Consolation* and signed on as crew mascot.

Perhaps the most unusual mascot of all is the mink kept by the first platoon of the 25th Military Police Company. If any lady applies for him to make part of a coat for herself, she's liable to be arrested.

If all those mascots came home together, they would make a transport look like a second Noah's Ark. When they do arrive, a hearty welcome awaits them and their masters.

GUNNER and the DUMBO

Story by Lt. Dwight W. Follett, U.S.N.R.
Pictures by Don Nelson

Coachwhip Publications
CoachwhipBooks.com

Coachwhip Publications
CoachwhipBooks.com

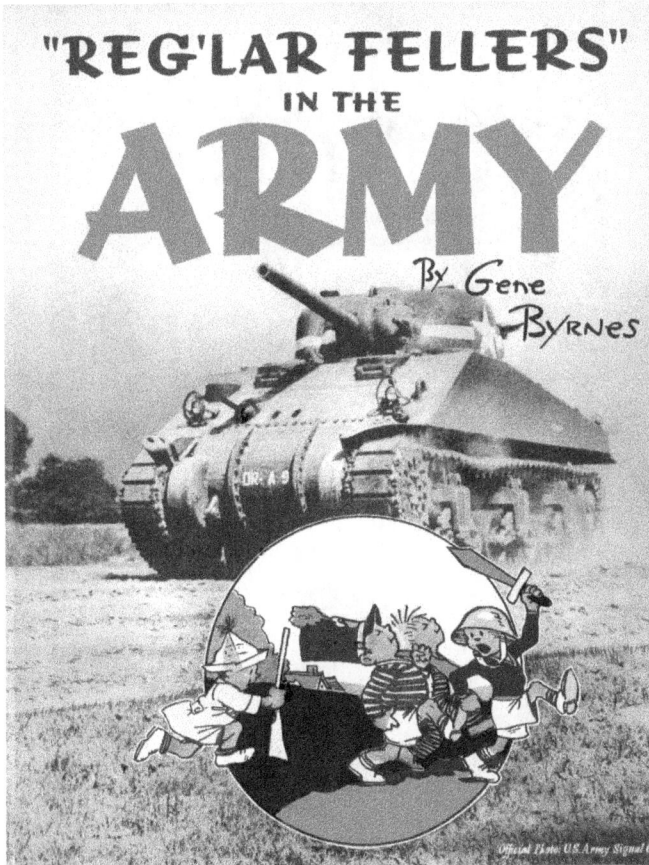

"REG'LAR FELLERS" IN THE ARMY By Gene Byrnes

Coachwhip Publications

CoachwhipBooks.com

PSYCHOLOGICAL WARFARE

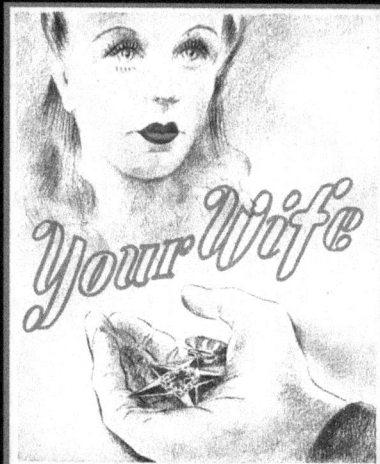

Your Wife

••• SHE WOULD PREFER YOUR SAFE RETURN

PAUL M. A. LINEBARGER

Coachwhip Publications
CoachwhipBooks.com

PAPER BULLETS
LEO J. MARGOLIN

Coachwhip Publications

CoachwhipBooks.com

BASTOGNE

The Story of the First Eight Days
In Which the 101st Airborne Division Was
Closed Within the Ring of German Forces

COLONEL S. L. A. MARSHALL

Coachwhip Publications
CoachwhipBooks.com

WAR
EAGLES

THE STORY OF THE EAGLE SQUADRON
by
JAMES SAXON CHILDERS
COLONEL, UNITED STATES ARMY AIR FORCES

Coachwhip Publications

CoachwhipBooks.com

MISSIE

THE LIFE AND TIMES OF

ANNIE OAKLEY

Annie Fern Swartwout

Coachwhip Publications

CoachwhipBooks.com

LAW AND ORDER. LTD.
THE LIFE OF ELFEGO BACA

Kyle S. Crichton

Coachwhip Publications
CoachwhipBooks.com

www.ingramcontent.com/pod-product-compliance
Lightning Source LLC
Chambersburg PA
CBHW081229090426
42738CB00016B/3236